S0-ABB-557

3 1491 00523 1976

TAKE CHARGE!

A "How-to" Approach
for Solving Everyday Problems

158.1 B219TA

BANNON, JOSEPH J.

TAKE CHARGE!

Niles Public
Library District

6960 Oakton Street
Niles, Illinois 60648
(708) 967-8554

SAC   61820

© 1992 Sagamore Publishing, Inc.

All rights reserved.

Interior design: Susan M. Williams
Cover design: Michelle R. Dressen
Editor: Lisa A. Busjahn
Proofreader: Phyllis L. Bannon

Library of Congress Catalog Card Number: 91-61668
ISBN: 0-915611-46-5

Printed in the United States of America

This book is dedicated to my father, a salesman personified. For over 30 years, he was the best cookie salesman in Glens Falls, New York. He saw to it that all the grocery stores were well stocked with Dane-t-Bits' Fig Newtons, Lady Fingers, and Kentucky Cremes.

Dane-T-Bits

CONTENTS

ACKNOWLEDGMENTS

A great many people have contributed to the writing of this book, far too many to name. During the last decade and a half, over twenty thousand individuals have participated in my problem-solving workshops . . . to them I owe a debt of gratitude. Their insights and meaningful suggestions have been invaluable. Thousands of individuals have used the problem-solving model in personal encounters as well as in organizational situations and they have shared their experiences. Over the years, many of my own colleagues have been particularly insightful and helpful. I could not have written these thoughts without them.

Special recognition is given to Susan Williams, who provided suggestions for formatting and writing style. Lisa Busjahn provided invaluable editing of the manuscript. Michelle Dressen made sense out of many of my thoughts in her design of the graphics used in the book. I'm also indebted to Phyllis Bannon, who serves as our "Human Spell Check."

Although my name appears as the author, this book couldn't have been written without the help and assistance of all of these individuals.

INTRODUCTION

This book was originally written as a textbook for managers in the public service. It was well received, selling over 25,000 copies. As a result of its success, I was invited to lecture and present workshops on problem solving. In the beginning, most of the participants were professionals in public service. The concept of the problem-solving process "caught on," and as a result, lay groups, volunteer groups, women's clubs, real estate personnel, and many nonprofessionals became participants in my workshops. I received many requests to put my ideas in writing and make them available to the general reader. This book is an attempt to do just that.

I draw on over 25 years of experience in teaching and in conducting problem-solving workshops. The problem-solving process presented here represents a seven-step procedure for solving everyday problems. It allows readers to take charge of their lives and the problems they face daily. It should be pointed out however, that nowhere in this book will you find any suggestion that problem solving is an easy task.

This book is not about magic—there are no special secrets! Problem solving requires perseverance and hard work. The reader should not infer that by following each step of the process all of his or her problems will be successfully solved! In order to become a successful problem solver, you must develop an attitude of constructive discontent and a desire to find a better way of doing things.

As I began to work with this process, I realized that planning alone was not the whole of the process. I became aware of the importance of being able to perceive forthcoming problems, and designing procedures to solve them. In a sense, solving problems is the very essence from which human endeavor is composed.

Throughout this book I have emphasized that it is essential to identify the *real* problem. If you do not identify the real problem, it is impossible to design solutions that eliminate the problems you face. What is often perceived as the *cause* of a problem is merely a *symptom* of a larger or more serious problem.

I have tried to emphasize that today's problems cannot be solved without using all of our creative instincts. Each of us has creative potential that with practice can be developed.

I examine the thought processes we use in decision making, and stress that the problem solver must accept full responsibility for the chosen solution. The work of problem analysis can be delegated, but the responsibility for decision making is ours.

It is my experience that great emphasis must be placed on the implementation of our ideas for solutions. Solutions are valuable only when we put them to use. Too many people are quick to come up with solutions, and slow to put them into action.

I have attempted to merge many of the conceptual and theoretical concepts of problem solving with practical application. No matter what your job: teacher, salesperson, volunteer, journalist, coach, secretary, or engineer, I believe the problem-solving process discussed here will be helpful to you in your everyday life.

*"Those who say they can't,
never will;
Those who say they can,
just might."*

Joseph J. Bannon

1

PUT YOURSELF IN CONTROL OF YOUR LIFE

"Being effective does not mean eliminating all of the problems in your life. It does mean moving your locus of control from the external to the internal. In that way you make yourself responsible for everything you experience emotionally."

Wayne Dyer

There are at least three things you can do to improve the quality of your daily life.

1.   *Become more in charge of yourself.*

2.   *Don't procrastinate.*

3.   *Set goals for what you want to achieve.*

As Wayne Dyer, author of *Your Erroneous Zones* says, truly intelligent people are in charge of themselves:

"They know how to choose happiness over depression, because they know how to deal with the problems of their lives. Notice I didn't say solve the problems. Rather than measuring their intelligence on their ability to solve the problem, they measure it on their capacity for maintaining themselves as happy and worthy, whether the problem gets solved or not" (p.9).

GAINING CONTROL OF YOUR LIFE

Being in control of yourself can make you a winner, even when you lose. Or, at least, it will keep you from falling apart if problems aren't solved to your satisfaction. Attempting to solve problems is as important as actually solving them. *Trying* to take control of some aspect of your life enhances healthful living.

Of course, knowing the difference between those aspects of life you can control — *problem situations* — and those you can't control — *fixed facts of existence* —is extremely important. By not confusing these two conditions, you'll be able to maintain some control over the achievable aspects of your life as well as over your reaction to others.

Thus, control is used in two distinct ways: to manage, remedy, or direct malleable (changeable) situations and to accept the fixed facts of existence. These are the hard and soft facts of life. Knowing the difference between a malleable situation and a fixed fact of existence has always been a hallmark of wisdom.

Your personal habits and attitudes have much to do with whether you retain or lose control over malleable events and situations in your life. Your attitudes, of course, are defined and shaped to a greater or lesser degree by your family, religious community, and social groups, as well as others.

Internal vs external control

When Dyer talks about internal *vs* external locus of control, he distinguishes two of our major perspectives. His terms are similar to those used in popular sociology to describe types of people: inner-directed or other-directed people; loners or group-oriented people; solitary or groupie people; unsociable or sociable people.

These two broad distinctions are now part of our popular literature and culture. In fact, you've probably already used these terms to describe people. You can be in either group, depending on the control you have over your life at any given moment. As early as 1912, Ernest Hocking recognized these distinctions and wrote in *The Meaning of God in Human Experience: A Philosophic Study of Religion:*

> "Any given moment of life people must choose between two goods, psychologically incompatible. On the one hand, the peace of the hermit, the silence of the forest, the exaltation of sacrifice, the mightiness of simplification and unity, the joy of self-abandonment, the calm of absolute contemplation. . . On the other hand, the variety and stress of life, the zest of common ends, the mastery of means, the glory of infinite enterprise, the pride of creativity and self-possession. The modern world as a whole has made its choice. But there is a better choice: namely, the choice of both. For the life of each is that it may lose itself, from time to time, in the life of the other. And this, which is obvious in things partial, is true—and even chiefly true, in things total" (p.427).

Nevertheless, such distinctions are useful if they help determine what type of person you are. Dyer, who actively favors the inner-directed person, believes that only 25 percent of Americans are internally motivated in their behavior. Internally motivated people's cues for behavior are self-determined and highly individualized. There is a good chance you aren't among this small percentage. If you are a self-reliant person, however, you might be surprised to discover that most people are not.

To be inner-directed does not mean you're shy or incapable of intimate and meaningful relationships. It basically means you look to yourself *first* for advice and judgment. It also doesn't mean that you seek *only* your own advice, but rather that your own perceptions and assessments carry a great deal of weight with you.

Independence and self-confidence

Trusting your own judgment is a learned behavior, as is not trusting it. Unlearning dependence on rules, regulations, values, and whims of others is the main topic of Dyer's book. Unlearning this dependence can aid you in dealing creatively with your everyday problems. Of course, unlearning behaviors and attitudes isn't as easy as learning them in the first place. But, unlearning behaviors and attitudes has been done by all kinds of people. Hocking stated in his book:

> "We do not begin as solitary beings and then acquire community: we begin as social products, and acquire the arts of solitude — a direction of progress more hopeful for variety and origination than a progress in the reverse direction" (p. 299).

Whether one is born other-directed, as Hocking believed, isn't critically important for our purposes. He is more interested in finer philosophic distinctions than we are here. What is important, however, is that most of us are under tremendous pressure from infancy onward to become "social products."

It's a rare child or young adult who is genuinely encouraged to look first to himself or herself as a source of guidance and strength. We've all heard self-reliance sentiments expressed, but when we were young, most of us were forced to follow and listen to others, especially adults. Even today we may encourage such dependency in our own children. I'm not speaking of the general guidance needed by children and young people. Rather, I am talking about the reluctance of many adults to let young people steadily outgrow their habits of instinctive reliance on the opinions or preferences of others.

Pressures that conspire to shape us into social products continue throughout life. Parents are joined by school officials, law enforcement agencies, employers, and other community and social groups to ensure that each individual considers the values and goals of groups or institutions as more important than his or her own.

Because it's actually simpler to consider others first, to live primarily for others than for oneself, most of us conform to these expectations. We're reinforced for being good children or good citizens, with social rewards for unquestioned loyalty. If you have little desire in developing beyond this model of social conformity, then you're probably a well-adjusted person, perhaps as well adjusted as any machine!

Problem Solving Tip #1

Develop your power to make your own assessments and choose your own values.

Joseph J. Bannon

For a group or society to survive, it needs our life-long involvement and consensus with its professed goals and values. Yet, what is demanded, but not required, is our unquestioned loyalty. History and our own experiences are filled with instances where thinking for oneself, based on one's own internal values, made a great difference in the outcome of events.

The opposite is even more evident. Group thinking or conformity to social, political, and military pressures has resulted in disastrous consequences. If independent, critical thinking is the root of civilized, free behavior, then it's certainly worth recapturing.

We may be subject to emotional cycles, but this doesn't mean we should surrender limply and use emotional cycles as an excuse for not trying. We aren't entirely puppets of this or of any other force. We can do many things to counteract them.

Self-reliance

Thinking for ourselves isn't easy, nor is it much encouraged in our everyday lives and training. Today, the message, *Work-it-out-yourself!* usually means we're supposed to find another authority figure or someone else to help us. The only self-reliance displayed in such cases is having just enough sense to get someone else to do whatever it is for us. Our dependency on experts and professionals isn't solely the result of a more complicated lifestyle. It's also a reflection of a learned or acquired disbelief in our own capacities.

With few exceptions, people did most things for themselves throughout most of human history. Now most things are done for us. While having others work for us wins time and leisure for more meaningful activities, it can also seriously undermine our trust in ourselves — unless we already have adequate confidence in our own experiences and abilities.

Distrust of the *jack-of-all-trades* approach has poisoned us as producers of our own needs. Instead, we specialize, considering it a substitute for wider knowledge and experience, which it isn't. The widespread interest and encouragement of folk art and crafts in this country may reveal not only a nostalgia for the past, but also a genuine hunger for hands-on skills in our everyday lives.

As passive consumers of goods and services, rather than producers or "prosumers" (the combination of producer and consumer Alvin Toffler describes as ideal in *The Third Wave*) we further accustom ourselves to dependence on others, and are applauded for doing so because we're considered realistic, community-oriented citizens. Perhaps in reality we're merely worshippers of the economy or some other false god.

Self-assessment and affirmation

One way of regaining control over our lives is to recapture those individual portions or potentialities that have been abandoned, knowingly or otherwise, to a group or family. You may be worried about becoming alienated from others if you begin to think and act more from your own impulses than from those to which you've conformed, compromised, or consented. But what about being alienated from yourself? Isn't that equally, or more serious?

Alienation from ourselves retards personal growth, undermines our relationships with others, and disables us for effective action in the world. The crucial "break" in the diagnosis of schizophrenia isn't with reality, but with sincerity. Although often incorrectly described as a break with outer reality, schizophrenia is a lack of connection with inner reality. If you're true to yourself, to paraphrase Shakespeare, you can then not be false to others.

For many it may be too late. Many people don't understand the desire for greater individuality or self-knowledge. To such people, the self may be a bothersome concept that frightens and threatens them with loneliness and isolation. They often find themselves relieved when there is a group or cause in which to lose themselves. Loss of self sometimes appears to be their objective.

Knowledge and acceptance of the self is a rock-bottom requirement if you wish to gain any degree of control over your life and its problems. To gain this knowledge you'll have to look within to determine how much is truly you, and how much are the acquired characteristics of a social product.

This isn't easy. In fact, it can be quite disturbing, but please don't rely exclusively on an expert to do it for you! We can get all sorts of help and guidance, but getting to know ourselves is initially a process of solitary assessment of who we are and what we really want. Some questions for a personal self-assessment follow.

- Do you make up your own mind or rely on others?

- Are you afraid to voice your opinions, and do you change them quickly if you encounter resistance?

- Are you easily frightened or overwhelmed by the demands of daily life?

- Do your own thoughts and dreams upset you? That is, are you ashamed or frightened of yourself? Do you even day-dream at all?

- Are you reluctant to be alone? Do you consider your behavior solely in terms of its likelihood of isolating you from others?

- Do you find emotional or psychological harmony in your life only when you're with others and in agreement with others?

- Is the approval of others necessary for you to embark on, or continue an activity? (This is, of course, within the range of legal activity.)

- Do you determine any of your own rules and regulations, especially in manners and morals?

- Do you like or love yourself? Do you accept the misconception that self-love is the same as being selfish, or that self-interested is the same as self-centered?

- Are you passive or active in response to the dilemmas and problems you face?

- Are you afraid of, or attracted to the new and unknown?

- Do you mind any amount of risk and uncertainty in your life?

- Are you compulsively routine or busy to avoid thinking about the meaning of life or your beliefs?

- Do you often feel guilty or anxious when you act spontaneously or independently without first checking with others?

- Do you know the good and bad aspects of both success and failure? Do you consider yourself a winner or loser on your own or someone else's terms?

- Do any of the above attitudes bother or please you? Do you wish to eliminate, expand, or change them?

In other words, do you have the habit of asking yourself why you do or don't do, feel or don't feel, think or don't think a certain way? How many of these behaviors are truly what you want, and how many are the result of conditioning and social pressure? You will begin to take control of yourself and your problems when you start answering questions such as those above.

Self-control

Don't be surprised if you're accused of being an amateur psychiatrist when you admit this self-analysis to others. Remind yourself that a major function of socialization is to keep you an amateur in most aspects of your life, so you will continue to require the assistance of "helping professions," as well as others.

Taking control of your life doesn't mean burying your temper or watching what you say. It means achieving control over those aspects of your life that have been controlled by others, either through default or weakness. There are plenty of situations in life over which we have no control without abdicating situations we can control! Like any self-initiated change, taking control can't be accomplished if we aren't willing to take chances.

People with full, enjoyable lives are not simply lucky. You can bet they have done and still do a lot to ensure its richness. Once you begin to take control over various areas of your life, you'll be surprised at how much that you thought was supposed to be controlled by the wills of others or destiny, really belongs in *your* hands.

To take control of your life is to get at the root of behaviors and attitudes that impede you. To accomplish this you must be a doer, not a procrastinator. Procrastination, or doing what is less important first, is a serious drawback in any quest for more creative living and effective problem solving.

IDENTIFYING PROCRASTINATION TACTICS

People who put things off don't gain peace of mind or leisure as a result. If they gain free time, it is invariably haunted by all that needs to be done — a load of work or decisions that become monsters in their own right.

Too much activity

People who put things off can be quite busy with other matters. In fact, one common delay tactic to justify procrastination is to claim you have business elsewhere. Being busy doesn't mean you're being effective, especially if you've avoided doing something that is essential to the performance of other tasks.

Procrastinators don't like to look back because that's where the crumbling foundations of their present lives are revealed. Occupying ourselves with small matters doesn't get at the poison of procrastination. We're simply creating a smoke screen when we engage in minor tasks to the point of exhaustion, with "no time" for more pressing concerns.

Because most of our daily actions and inactions are interrelated, procrastination can impede the smooth functioning of the rest of our lives. You can't get the laundry done if you haven't fixed the washing machine. You can't lead an orderly life if your clothes are dirty. This example can be carried as far as we like.

Procrastination serves many purposes. We don't procrastinate against our will. Its cancerous development is encouraged because it allows us to avoid risk, uncertainty, and change in our lives. No matter how bored and restless we are, too often we remain with the familiar and put off what should or could be done. Our jobs, family lives, and friendships may have gone stale long ago. Yet we put off having to deal with these directly to avoid the risk of failure, not realizing that the biggest failure is procrastination. When others do for us what we've neglected, we're reinforced in our procrastination.

Problem Solving Tip #2

Develop your tools for happiness: thought, organization, action, and disdain for procrastination.

Joseph J. Bannon

William Knaus wrote in *Do It Now*:

"People whose style is that of mental procrastination often comment upon how unhappy they are, focus too hard on trying to rid themselves of negative feelings, and routinely repeat procrastination patterns. They suffer from disorganized thinking, obsessive ruminations, and indecisiveness."

Addictive behaviors

Procrastination can be a serious block to problem solving. Its symptoms may include boredom and dependency on drugs, alcohol, tobacco, or other distractions. We become bored when we do nothing to change our lives. Boredom leads to dissatisfaction with the way things are. Too often we blame others for our problems, instead of looking to ourselves for a change.

Procrastination can confound the symptoms of deeper problems. We may decide to embark on a diet, decrease our television time, or eliminate our consumption of alcohol, tobacco, and other drugs, because any one of these addictions may seem to be the root of our problem. After all, we think, if we weren't overweight, or groggy from drink, or less rushed for time and so forth, then we would certainly get important things done.

Of course, we'd be healthier if we'd give up, or at least reduce, our dependency on these crutches. However, that alone won't keep us from procrastinating. Addictions can be merely part of an arsenal of procrastination tactics to avoid more serious underlying problems. Giving up smoking by chewing on a stick of gum doesn't alleviate the need for oral activity, even though it rids your body of narcotics.

The art of achievement

Problem solving, or the attempt to deal with problems, is the art of getting at something. Procrastination is its opposite. It is a tactic of avoidance, of not getting at the root of a problem. In writing about inner-directed people, Dyer describes them as persons who grow their own roots in new or novel situations. I view a procrastinator as someone who is unaware of roots entirely, be they physical, psychological, emotional or otherwise. A procrastinator rarely thinks about being able to establish new roots or patterns of growth.

As well as being vulnerable to becoming substance abusers, procrastinators are often great consumers and abusers of time. They waste time worrying about what has been left undone, or the consequences of leaving matters unfinished. They waste time justifying delay tactics to themselves and others. Underlying causes for failure to act usually get lost in the surface confusion or boredom of such living. Just like any other addiction, procrastination is a weakness or disorder that leads us to avoid taking control of our lives.

BREAKING THE HABIT OF PROCRASTINATION

Do something you've been putting off. That's the first step to breaking the habit of procrastination. One step leads to another. The first step is undoubtedly the most difficult, especially if you've been putting it off for a long time.

Those who are doers know that even brief attention to what needs doing, if applied faithfully and properly, gets the job done. Doers connect actions to one another in a relay fashion. Soon they have a chain of movement toward their goals. This momentum can be yours once *you* undertake a task and move toward a goal.

As we discussed earlier, the momentum of information gathering can teach you how to solve problems. The more action you take on a problem, the more you learn about it, the better you get at solving it. This experience has its own momentum, regardless of the nature of the task or problem. You acquire the skill of tackling problems head-on as soon as they appear, by starting things in motion that may solve a problem, by working on related problems or tasks simultaneously, and by gaining confidence in your ability to control your life.

You become faster and faster in this process as you run the relay again and again. Soon the steps of the problem-solving model become automatic as you accomplish tasks, solve problems, and meet objectives. This doesn't happen magically for you, rather it comes about through your own efforts and commitment.

Many people get ill or sleepy at the thought of doing disagreeable tasks, such as mowing the lawn, fixing a furnace, examining our weaknesses, or even writing a book! It might be wonderful to enjoy more leisure; however, one of the necessities of a full, healthy life is to do work that is meaningful and varied. To be physically and mentally happy, most of us must overcome inertia to run a relay toward a specific goal.

You may have observed that the people who relish life and seem happy most of the time are the same people who enjoy disagreeable tasks. This glow may come from a sense of duty fulfilled, or from religious motivation, but I like to think the glow is from experiencing the sense of accomplishment that a job well done provides. Happy people probably draw on a wealth of job-completed experiences when their energy or interest lags.

Doing can replace the habit of not doing to the degree that you may run the risk of becoming a workaholic! Giving up one addiction for another isn't our aim. We want to free ourselves of all unhealthy dependencies, including taking on too many tasks. The goal is to be neither apathetic nor driven in activities, but to be in control. Control is a state of balance and equilibrium.

Even if others praise or excuse our addiction to inactivity or activity, whatever distracts us from self-knowledge and self-accomplishment is a loss to us. Develop the habit of thinking for yourself, and you'll be able to resist the pull of group inertia and group hysteria.

ACQUIRING THE HABIT OF GOAL ACHIEVEMENT

Acquiring the habit of setting and reaching goals is the easiest of the basic self-management skills to master. Setting goals can motivate you to work toward a specific aim or in a general direction. Even in this more simple area of self-control, we come across the difference between inner-motivated and externally motivated people.

"... highly external persons feel they are at the mercy of the environment, that they are being manipulated by outside forces and their goals are externally determined. If they set goals, they tend to be short-range ones. Internally motivated persons, on the other hand, feel they are in control; they are 'free' to set goals, think in terms of the future and long-range goals. They can both adapt the environment and adapt to it" (Paolucci, pp.132).

People who habitually look to others for advice and guidance and worry about what others will say or think, find any attempt at goal setting difficult. They're usually confined to developing short-range goals because they fear wider possibilities. Externally-oriented people are also fearful of their surroundings and environment. They tend to blame others, and assume that fate or destiny determines their lives.

For general problem solving, dealing with procrastination, or developing self-discipline, setting goals can be immensely useful. Such goals are somewhat different from the goals and objectives decided on in solving a problem. First try to tackle the personal daily planning habits that get things done. Without these, setting larger or longer-range goals is difficult or impossible.

Goals can be simple or complex. If you haven't been in the habit of setting goals for yourself, start by developing simple goals. Once you begin to set and achieve goals, the habit of planning ahead will become familiar and pleasant. To rid yourself of one habit — such as a lack of direction in your activities and behavior — substitute a positive habit. Two contradictory habits won't exist together for long. One inevitably will triumph over the other. Attempting to discard a habit without substituting an alternative in its place is more difficult.

By goal setting and modifying goals that turn out to be impossible to achieve, you'll have a map to refer to as you travel toward what you want. Step by step you can reach higher or longer-range goals if you plan carefully. You can't climb a ladder without taking the first step.

Most of us need to plan ahead, consider the consequences carefully, and then proceed. You can decide to begin to set goals now just as you can decide to stop procrastinating now. In fact, you can combine these decisions into one goal: *Today I will stop procrastinating on a specific task or action.* You already set a goal for yourself by deciding to read this book. Count that achievement to your credit!

I've set retroactive goals for myself, glancing back on what I've already accomplished and giving myself overdue credit for it. This helps to relieve me of some of my frustration when I face a new problem. Having recognized an accomplishment, you may be more able to develop another goal or get moving on one you already have. For example, after you give yourself credit for reading this book, set a new goal — to put many of the suggestions offered in these pages to work in your life.

Goal setting can be accomplished by using a simple form of the *To-Do* list. This list can be confined to one overall goal — such as attaining a college degree or a leave of absence from work — or it can encompass your daily and long-range goals. Here is one type of *To-Do* list:

IMMEDIATE:

> Get appointment for:
> Call:
> See:
> Write:
> Start Plans for:

INTERMEDIATE:

> Check status of:
> Follow-up on:
> Consider beginning:
> Be prepared for:

LONG RANGE:

> Seek a new:
> Create a different:
> Start building a:
> Consider modifying the:

My *To-Do* list is a combination of "now," "later," and "if-ever" goals.

- Do shopping and other weekly errands.

- Take pets for annual check-up.

- Have several chapters of this book retyped.

- Repaint my old toolbox.

- Clean out heavy items from the garage loft; put permanent jack under it to raise sagging roof.

- Get mending and laundry done.

- Plan for garden/order seeds, etc.

- Get this book published.

- Call doctor for medical check-up.

The benefits of goal setting will soon be evident to you, because your level of efficiency and productivity will increase. You'll probably feel better and become more fully able to enjoy your leisure as well. You'll seldom waste time or spin your wheels if you have specific goals you're working on. Nor will your free time be full of worry about what you haven't done.

If you have some unexpected time, you can choose to relax, or to work on something on your *To-Do* list. The greatest feeling of all is the joy of getting things accomplished because you now have control of your time and life.

2

WHY SOLVE PROBLEMS?

*"To live is to have problems,
and to solve problems is
to grow intellectually."*

J.P. Guilford

When we think of problem-solving techniques, we often think of methods used by experts working in large industries or for governmental agencies. Just as entrepreneurs and politicians are responsible for providing solutions to broad economic and social problems, we are responsible for solving the problems in our own lives. We know that comfort cannot be purchased or legislated.

Solutions to everyday problems are reached as a result of our abilities to act out habitual and healthful responses. Problems come in all sizes. We have major difficulties and daily situations that call for one decision after another. We make these decisions according to the good or bad habits that we've developed solving problems through the years.

Everyone has problems. They might lie with our jobs, health, school, careers, families, clubs, or group activities, or in our relationships with others. With the fast pace of today's life, many of us face several important problems all at once! Each stage of life brings new problems or changes that make it necessary to adjust previously made decisions. We are obligated to make up our minds on matters concerning home life, work, community activities, and even organizational and governmental issues.

Some decisions are automatically made, with little conscious effort or thought. We make countless decisions daily that permit us to function effectively, without spending much time on them. This automatic decision-making process is similar to the reactions our bodies have to a constant array of physical changes and challenges.

At times, life runs smoothly without much conscious thought on issues related to our physical or social well being. However, the occurrence of such mind and body poise is so rare that it is the goal of many religious and practical philosophies. Though we don't necessarily want to strive for philosophic poise, we *do* want to be able to solve everyday problems as smoothly and effectively as possible.

KNOWING WHEN A PROBLEM EXISTS

In simplest terms, a problem exists when we have difficulty reaching a desired outcome or goal. We know what it is we want to achieve, either alone, or with the help of others. We know the outcome or compromise that we desire in the case of a particular problem.

It's very important in everyday living to be able to recognize a problem when it exists. Regardless of the seriousness of a particular problem, you may sometimes find that you want to avoid it more than anything else. You may not even admit to yourself that there *is* a problem. Maybe you feel overwhelmed by problems or simply unable to cope. A head-in-the-sand approach might be the only solution needed or wanted until the problem becomes too serious or obvious to avoid.

Not facing problems or not admitting they exist doesn't mean that you're lazy. Often we avoid solving problems because we don't know what to do. When we avoid problems, we don't give ourselves the chance to learn any new problem-solving skills. Apathy in the face of problems may be due to a lack of self-confidence rather than laziness. Sometimes a *"Why-bother?"* attitude is based on personal cynicism. This attitude expands if we allow many problems to go unsolved.

Reluctant problem solvers may not realize that experience teaches, even if the experience is failure. We can learn much from our failures. It's important to remember that the *process of trying* is healthful, helpful, and life-enhancing. If you try to enjoy and learn by exercising your problem-solving skills, your *"Why-bother?"* attitude will fade. In fact, problem solving is similar to physical exercise in that the more you do it, the greater the reward, both physically and mentally.

UNDERSTANDING BARRIERS TO PROBLEM SOLVING

There are many barriers to effective problem solving, but you can learn to expose and confront them as you begin to focus on a particular problem. To help you become aware of barriers that can block your way to utilizing resources and opportunities that could help you solve problems, I've listed several common obstacles.

Prejudice

We all have some prejudices. Everyone has heard — or even said — some variation of prejudices like these:

> Ladies don't do that.
> Children shouldn't see that.
> He's too old, or too young, or too —————— for that.

These are examples of barriers that can stop us in our tracks. To break the prejudice barrier and transform a *"Why-bother?"* or *"I-wouldn't-dare!"* attitude to a *"Why-not?"* attitude, you need to see your problem as a challenge. Challenges are obstacles to overcome, or opportunities to achieve desired goals. Problems are loaded with negative baggage. Challenges are not.

Problem Solving Tip #3

Being methodical increases the efficiency of our actions by preventing delays, avoiding waste of effort and reducing the risk of making mistakes.

K. F. Jackson

We need to drop the weights of prejudice and take the first positive steps in problem solving. We are much closer to successful problem solving if we reduce the clutter of useless mental and emotional barriers. We're then able to see problems as opportunities to gain self-confidence, as well as to reach solutions.

Ridicule

Ridicule is another barrier to problem solving. Ridicule is a fear of what others might say or think, and is related to prejudice. Ridicule can come from family, friends, co-workers, or other acquaintances. If you fear ridicule—real or imagined—you may prevent yourself from trying to solve a problem. The fear of ridicule is a dragon usually nourished in our minds. It needs to be confronted directly. By not allowing this fear to stop you, you free yourself to do something real about your problem and to gain confidence in the process. If you avoid problem solving because of fear of ridicule, you carry a double burden: the problem that probably won't disappear, and the bundle of unnecessary fears that feed on themselves.

Insecurity

Insecurity stems from a lack of self-confidence, and may retard your problem-solving efforts. You may be afraid that you'll lose something or someone if you act on a problem. Fear of the consequences, regardless of the solution you reach, may also dampen your enthusiasm and *commitment* to solving a problem. If you make a decision to act on a belief or a principle, or to solve a problem, you may upset those you need and love. Fear of consequences shouldn't dictate your behavior. Think about those who will be affected by your decision, but remember that the burden of deciding is yours. Loss is a normal part of life.

Lack of motivation or resources

Aside from these fears or prejudices, you may lack *motivation* or *resources* to solve a problem. If you can't see that solving a problem will make any difference, you lack motivation. If you don't have the money or time to undertake a problem — or don't think that you do — you may not even try to tackle any part of it. In either of these cases, you must remember to view a problem as a challenge, or an opportunity to gain experience and skills. This perspective will weaken the barriers that seem insurmountable. If a problem is worth solving, and you feel you're the only person to do it, your motivation will increase, and you will find the ability, the time, or the money to do it!

Dependency on others or personal crisis

You may be dominated by a group, such as your family, co-workers, or other club members. They can also disable you in independent decision making. You may wish to avoid the jealousy of others by avoiding any decision that might cause envy or resentment. Or you may be retarded by confusion, a bad time in your life, poor health, a divorce, declining physical strength, or some other negative factor.

Lack of self-discipline

Lack of self-discipline can cause us to be slow to react when a task needs to be accomplished, and this also creates barriers. Negativism, or complacency, or depending too much on others to make decisions all interfere with successful problem solving.

Lack of knowledge

Finally, lack of knowledge about a particular problem or situation may be a real or imagined barrier. With some commitment and motivation, however, just as with time and money, the necessary knowledge can often be acquired. Or you can determine who can help you solve a problem, and that's a form of knowledge in itself. It might be a friend, teacher, your doctor, or another skilled professional.

We can make a habit of ignoring problems, or of learning to solve them. Although not all problems can be solved, the problems most of us encounter daily on the job, at home, and with friends and associates are usually solvable with some remedy or compromise. Ignoring a problem accomplishes nothing, and may actually damage the situation further.

You are lucky if you were taught as a child to face and resolve difficulties. If a parent or guardian can't face problems, the child will probably not learn to either. Thus, there are two good reasons for wanting to become a more effective problem solver: to enhance your own life, and to be a worthwhile role model to others, especially young people.

MANAGING YOUR TIME FOR
SUCCESSFUL PROBLEM SOLVING

Finding the time to deal with your problems is a key step in problem solving. When you effectively manage your time, you decrease your level of stress, and therefore waste less time on stress-related accidents, quarrels, illnesses, and fatigue. Medical studies indicate that untreated stress can cause ulcers, heart disease, and high blood pressure. Long-term stress can cause emotional and psychological ailments such as severe depression. In the rest of this chapter, we'll look at some other steps you can take to clear your desk and your mind for problem solving.

Most of the problems you face (or avoid) are manageable. Some start out as "bite-sized" problems, but if you avoid them for any of the above reasons, they usually grow and get worse with time. You might be too busy even to focus on a problem, let alone give it proper attention. You may believe you don't have time to solve problems, even after admitting to their presence. So you're not really consciously avoiding or trying to escape problems, you simply believe you cannot solve them.

How do problems become manageable? Finding time is sometimes the first step. Whether you're time-poor or time-rich, the management of time is essential for successful problem solving. Time is needed to get things done, to think about problems, and to view any situation in perspective or context. Rushing into a problem situation with limited time for thought or action could make matters worse. A *"Doing something-is-better-than-nothing"* attitude isn't effective when facing issues that demand care and attention.

Problem Solving Tip #4

There are no gimmicks or shortcuts. Sloppy time management is just like a bad habit. You must be committed to doing something about it . . . the same as losing weight, or stopping smoking, or beating a drug habit.

J.D. Ferner

Time management is like ecology: pressure or relief in one area affects everything else in some way. It's foolish to complain about not having time, because complaining wastes time, and you'll have nothing to show for it. Few of us are attracted to unhappy or dissatisfied people. Complaining often frightens off people who could be helpful in a problem-solving situation!

And, the problem we tried to avoid by complaining about it still claims our time.

If the roof leaks, ignoring it won't make it go away. You could spend time worrying about it, mopping water, carrying buckets, and protecting interiors. On the other hand, you could try to fix the leak—*solve the problem*—and save time and anxiety. We can all think of times in our own lives or in the lives of our friends, when ecological interrelationships got out of hand simply because of poor time management.

Time management is really the management of all activities we engage in during our lives. Time logs and other written records are helpful for managing time more efficiently. An hour of planning will save many hours of correcting mistakes, as well as time otherwise wasted on unimportant activities with low priorities. Learn to get more benefit from your time by asking yourself three key questions:

- **Where does my time go?**
- **Where *should* my time go?**
- **How can I use my time better?**

The first step is to examine how you actually spend time. Keep a time log. List the major activities or events that cause you to waste time and how much time you spend on them. You'll probably discover two revealing facts:

1. **You're probably spending 80 percent of your time on activities that produce only 20 percent of actual benefit.**

2. **You may create your own time-wasters, or other people may generate them for you.**

Determining priorities is critical. Rank each activity you do. Assign an "A" to items of high priority, a "B" to those of moderate priority, and a "C" to low-priority items. When you begin your day, start with the "A's" and not with the "C's." Complete the most important tasks first. When the list is complete, prepare an action plan to achieve each goal. Use a *To-Do* list for unusual or complex projects. Getting a handle on time management may take some time and patience. We tend to work on minor tasks first, with the intention of leading up to larger projects. What often happens is that the more difficult jobs don't get done, simply because too much time is spent on unimportant activities.

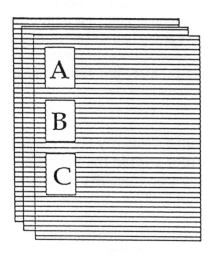

Well-managed time will allow you to guide and encourage others, while winning for yourself the precious hours for planning, rest, and for generally viewing your life in a broader context. The following tips on time management will help you achieve such leisure:

Keep an up-to-date To-Do list of everything you want to complete each day or week. Revise the list regularly, reordering the importance of various tasks, crossing off items that have been completed, are no longer necessary, or have been delegated. Don't spend too much time or deliberation on the list. Use it to map out your day (or week) in advance, consulting it faithfully as a refresher, and drawing lines through completed tasks. It is very reinforcing to use this simple method if you are faithful to the habit. However, avoid any tendency to become a compulsive list-maker instead of a doer. Reviewing your list should be done in a minor and automatic way, so that you can methodically clear the decks each day. The list is like a table of contents for your life's work.

Use any spare time to clear away busywork. Delegate busywork to another person. Delegate the small as well as the large projects.

Use all available technology effectively. This includes travel and office devices such as phones, computers, word-processors and dictation equipment. If you travel by car, have these items in duplicate.

Don't put off an important task because it's unpleasant. Attack all tasks without prejudice or favor. Force yourself to get into the habit of doing each day not only what you like, but also what you dislike.

Do the right job at the right time. Don't clean out your files when you should be preparing a report. Try to recognize when you are avoiding a distasteful responsibility.

Set personal and business priorities. "For every hour you plan, you save four," according to Susan Silver of "Positively Organized!", Santa Monica, California. Put your priorities in order on your *To-Do* list.

Guard your time. Set aside fixed times at home or work when you cannot be interrupted. This will not be easy if you work in an organization or atmosphere that administers by crises, or inflates every event into a crisis.

Reduce paperwork. Do one of the following immediately: For every piece of paper you handle, throw it away, refer it to someone, file it, or do what it requests. The best habit for correspondence is to answer your mail daily.

Get in the habit of making decisions. Almost any decision is better than unnecessary delay, especially on matters that aren't critical. Delegate less critical matters so they won't be brought to your attention.

Take the first step. Begin poking holes in a task or project: get *started* by listing the people you need to contact for information, or by gathering together files and other information, or by preparing an outline.

Set deadlines for yourself. Tell others about the deadlines to motivate you to meet them on time.

Learn to say No *as well as* Yes. Unless you're a rare person who is more productive when busy or pressured, you won't get anything done if you agree to do too much.

Finish projects and tasks. Completing a few jobs is better than leaving many jobs incomplete or dangling.

Being time-rich does not in itself mean you'll be an effective problem solver. If you lack experience and confidence in solving problems, you'll just have a lot more time to waste. If you're unemployed or work at home, you can attest to this! In fact, the busier you are, the more efficient you may be. Some kinds of pressures stimulate achievement and productivity. Have you ever heard the adage that if you want something done, ask a busy person? This saying was probably coined because busy people have usually learned how to manage time so that every minute counts. Most busy people also know how and when to relax and aren't at the mercy of the clock.

DISTINGUISHING SYMPTOMS
FROM THE REAL PROBLEM

Personal problems are often more manageable because they are your own. They're not occurring elsewhere, beyond your influence, but rather are within the scope of your everyday responsibilities and desires. Personal problems are right under your nose, often obvious to you and others. They may involve some aspect of your home life (children, spouse, or lover), friendships, career or retirement plans, or financial considerations.

You know best what aspects of your life might be causing stress. Once you have identified the source of stress (or any other sign or symptom), the best approach is to analyze it further. You're fortunate if you have only *one* problem. However, if that one problem is ignored or neglected, it may develop into a cluster of problems that demand attention. It then becomes critically important to recognize the *symptoms* of a problem, and separate them from the problem itself.

A symptom is the result of a problem, not the cause. Water is not the problem with a leaky roof — the problem is what causes the hole and how to seal it. In some cases, minor problems are symptoms of a much larger problem. Don't be put off by this, because the bigger the problem you solve, the greater the benefit. If the leak in the roof is caused by overhanging tree limbs that periodically damage the roof, trimming back the tree will reduce future problems; whereas sealing the hole will only be a temporary solution. In this case, the damaged roof is actually a symptom of a greater problem.

Take, for example, the problem of an automatic garage door manufacturer as described by C.H. Kepner and B.B. Tregoe in their book, *The Rational Manager*. The manufacturer's garage door was powered by a tiny radio transmitter in the user's car that activated the door, raising or lowering it as needed. The transmitter had an ultrashort range, so that one signal wouldn't raise all the garage doors in the block.

When the doors were first introduced they were very successful. But in autumn that year, as the weather turned cooler and fog began to roll in from the bay, complaints began to roll into the company: "Darned thing came right down on the middle of my new convertible, and I didn't touch the transmitter button!"

The company faced a major crisis and proceeded to investigate the problem. Examination showed that the complaints were made on certain foggy days, but not on others. Further specification showed that the complaints usually came in late afternoon and evening. As company personnel plotted the sources of the complaints on a city map, they realized they came primarily from a single area on a strip of land that extended into the bay, cutting entirely across the residential section of the point. This strip was wider at the ocean end and narrower at the bay end.

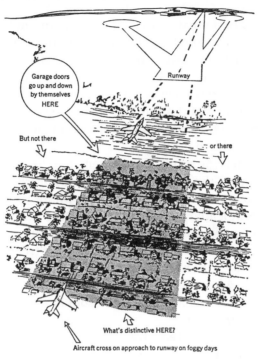

Aircraft cross on approach to runway on foggy days

Once the problem area had been identified, company personnel started searching for distinctions in the specifications. They asked themselves (and others) what happened on those days when there were complaints, as opposed to days when there were no complaints. As stated, complaint days were foggy days. What was distinctive about late afternoon and early evening? When there *was* fog, this was the time when the fog rolled in.

What was distinctive about the narrow, cone-shaped strip of land from which the complaints came? This strip lined up with a Naval Air Station runway located on an island out in the bay. Planes crossed that strip of land as they made their final approach. Thus the distinctions in the specifications were fog in the air and planes crossing this area on their final approach to the longest runway. Now, what actually happened?

During the foggy periods, the Naval Air Station flight controller guided the aircraft into landings by radar using a special radio frequency. He also used the longest runway exclusively for ground-controlled approaches. Aircraft coming in over the strip of land on foggy days also used the same special radio frequency. A check on this frequency proved it to be the same as the frequency used to operate the garage doors. Every time the Naval flight controller and an incoming pilot spoke to each other during an approach, their radio frequency would run the doors up and down!

After this discovery, everyone recalled that all the doors had opened or shut at the same time, that there was always a plane overhead, and that it was always foggy at the time. No one initially recognized that these factors combined to create the problem, because their experiences didn't help them to see the pertinent facts. The door manufacturer changed the mechanisms to a new frequency, and the trouble disappeared.

In this case, if the manufacturer had sent out workers to repair mechanisms immediately after receiving the complaints, the company would have been treating the *symptoms* instead of the *real problem*. Although identifying and treating the real problem initially took more thought and time, doing so saved time, money, and the company's reputation. As individuals, though, we should put limits on the time we spend searching for larger problems. This is necessary to avoid getting stuck in a mental swamp, and becoming disabled for real problem solving. We must try to look beyond the symptoms, or separate the symptoms from the problem in the first place.

It is usually best to solve one problem at a time, rather than a cluster of them. It is even wiser, however, to focus on a major problem first, if it breeds the others. Regardless of how you solve your problem, the worst thing to do is nothing. Living with pressure without attempting to ease it means living with long-term anxiety or fear. The body's response to such tension and uncertainty can be permanent physical or emotional disability.

Effective problem-solving skills, which lie within your reach, can help you lead a healthier, more fulfilling, and satisfying life. Of course, education is important for effective problem solving, but don't forget that education comes in both formal and informal ways. You can *learn* to solve problems, or you can *acquire* these skills through experience. Chapter Three will discuss when formal education can help you, and when it cannot. Lack of schooling is no excuse for a lack of problem-solving skills, when you can learn by doing.

3

THINKING CREATIVELY

*"We are shut up in schools and colleges
. . . for ten or fifteen years, and come out
at last with a bellyful of words and do not
know a thing."*

Ralph Waldo Emerson

Many people don't understand their thinking processes, or how they *could* think about the problems they need to solve. Problem solving is an essential skill that has been virtually lost in the gap between home and formal education. If the habit of solving problems as they occurred was not part of your home upbringing, you probably didn't acquire the habit through formal education either.

Few courses or teachers train students in practical, everyday decision making and problem solving. Educators usually ignore these basic skills, presuming they will somehow be acquired in the home or elsewhere, and parents assume teachers are instructing their children in methods of solving everyday problems.

DEFINING THE THINKING GAP

An integration of formal education and home learning is difficult to achieve, yet such a combination is necessary to prepare children to become capable adults, able to cope with life's demands. Ideally, the problem-solving abilities that one form of education ignores, the other should provide instruction in. That ideal rarely exists, however, because parents and schools continually debate their responsibilities. Because this question of responsibility is far from settled, those growing up during times of rapid change and uncertainty may find it especially difficult to face change and the problems that change can bring.

Even the periodic call for a return to the basics in education doesn't emphasize the need to pass along problem-solving skills. Teachers, students, and employers agree that reading, writing, and computing skills are necessary components in a well-rounded education today. Educators agree that there is a need to encourage creative thinking as well.

How to think is so essential and so basic a skill that educators and parents mistakenly assume that it comes naturally to a growing child, as though it were an untutored instinct. Many of us know adults who don't seem to ever think about anything but the simplest matters. They were probably never taught to think analytically. Analytical thinking is dramatically different from the memorization or any other discipline taught in most public and private schools. Those who haven't been trained to problem solve at any level of their educational experience are usually unaware of the skills they are missing.

Employers are keenly aware of our educational system's failures. However, they put little pressure on schools to improve, because they expect to have to train or retrain employees. Educators, especially in higher grades, complain to other teachers and parents about the minimal competency levels demonstrated by young people in basic skills. Parents also complain — often to educators. The students, who are often forgotten in this debate, might actually learn something if the issue of inadequate skills was approached as a problem to be solved.

The purpose of formal education is to prepare young people to adjust to society's mores. To a lesser extent, this is also the goal of family life. Educating young people to take on fixed roles makes little sense in a society that is changing as rapidly as ours does. Children and young people should be educated to be adaptable and responsive to change. Even if we desire a return to traditional values, young people are cheated today if flexibility in thought and action is not part of their education.

NARROWING THE THINKING GAP

Don't despair if you—like millions of other "educated" people—don't feel adequately educated. You may feel you managed to graduate into adult life without being fully prepared for its complex and shifting demands. Perhaps we all expect too much or too little from education. But that's a question for another book. The difficulty you may have now in generating effective and creative solutions can be remedied.

One way to teach yourself to think effectively and creatively, is to remember what it was like to be a child. In *Maximum Life Span*, Roy L. Walford, M.D., quotes British film director Nicolas Roeg, on "The Man Who Fell to Earth." He writes that this film was "best understood by the under-12 and the over-80. They had no problems with it because the very old have gone past cultural conditioning. They don't care anymore. And the young do not yet have preconceptions, which can be so binding."

Walford believes that conditions that encourage or allow very young people to be open to change and exploration may reappear among the elderly. The elderly who "no longer care" aren't merely apathetic or despondent. The carefree tranquility Walford observed among the very elderly is actually quite inspiring: "Very old individuals are often quite wonderfully tranquil, serene, self-motivated, and, what is most pertinent to our futurist inquiry, pleasingly and stubbornly independent, even radical."

Because you're probably among those of us who are over 12 years old and under 80 years old, your best source of natural encouragement for creative thinking will come from youthful memories gained during the time before your imagination was curbed and trained. Albert Einstein said, "Imagination is more important than knowledge, for knowledge is limited, whereas imagination embraces the entire world — stimulating progress, giving birth to evolution."

Even as a very young boy, Einstein had learned to trust his "inner voice" more than he did authority and convention. He cherished and defended that trust. If we want to become creative problem solvers, we have to rediscover our inner voices and renew our trust in what they have to tell us. Many creativity and problem-solving consultants encourage their clients to throw off layers of cultural conditioning, and to go beyond the boundaries of lock-step thinking by incorporating exercises that stimulate child-like spontaneity. A cover story in the usually conservative *Business Week* reviewed such creativity sessions for business leaders:

> "Participants learn a variety of exercises intended to get their creative juices flowing. Using devices from the "chicken cheer" to flying kites, creative consultants try to break down rigid thinking that blocks new ideas. And with a grab bag of techniques from fantasy to thumbing through the dictionary, they try to imbue their grey-flannel pupils with a bit of the stuff that made an Einstein or a Mozart" (September 30, 1985, p. 80).

Creativity consultants and advisers often feel that formal education limits rather than encourages creativity. In fact, modern education, which stresses logic, seems to squelch creativity. Research indicates that a child's creativity plummets dramatically between the ages of five and seven. By the age of 40 most adults are only about two percent as creative as they were at age five. Some college education may foster creativity, but experts believe that graduate school may perpetuate entrenched thinking in some fields.

Fortunately, some school systems are reacting to these criticisms by introducing creativity training into secondary school curricula. However, it is badly needed at the elementary level as well. It makes little sense to stifle creativity at the lower levels only to attempt to restimulate it in the upper grades.

Problem Solving Tip #5

Assume that you don't know everything, that new opportunities surround you, waiting to be discovered, and that your opinions are obsolete.

Joseph J. Bannon

Robert Olson, author of *The Art of Creative Thinking—A Practical Guide*, says that creative people can live with the uncertainty of not knowing all the answers. They are more concerned about improving their field of interest than favorably impressing others. They seek to organize their experience and ideas and bring meaning into them.

There is much you can do to free yourself from the habit of thinking as others do. By reassessing the more traditional (and uninspired) ways of thinking, you can begin to revive your own imagination. For example, both your formal and informal education may have taught you to approach ideas too narrowly and timidly. This is especially noticeable in times of accelerated change and progress. Once you begin to trust your own solutions to problems, you start to stretch the boundaries of your imagination. And the more you seek or imagine solutions to problems, the more creative you're likely to become.

Remember, experiences generate further thought and action. Formal education and learning only provide intentionally limited and "precoded" types of experiences. According to Alvin Toffler in *Future Shock,* such pre-engineered messages tend to be "tighter, more condensed, less redundant" instead of "loose or carelessly framed." In other words, information and images are often stripped of the variety and complexity of informal communication.

As stated earlier, the purpose of most schools is to educate people to fit into society, and "fitting in" is generally incompatible with creativity and imagination. As a society, we wish on the one hand to have stability, and on the other, to have innovation. Einstein's loyalty and dedication to his own genius and imagination are rare qualities and require a tremendous amount of courage and stamina. Far too often most of us experience a kind of "intellectual schizophrenia" between our more natural uncoded sources of information and what is officially acceptable.

When I speak of sparking or stimulating your imagination and creativity, I do so fully recognizing the opposition you'll probably encounter. Many groups and organizations, including businesses, tend to smother creative thinking among individual members. Although most employers claim they're constantly seeking new solutions to problems, the effort employees often have to make to get an idea through the maze of office bureaucracy to someone who can approve or implement it, is so exhausting that many don't persevere. Their innovative ideas then die a quiet death.

The cost of creativity in most organizations and groups is high. The person who is inquisitive or looks for new ideas seems to be "rocking the boat," and is often difficult to influence. To others, he or she appears rebellious and uncooperative.

Creative thought invariably induces change, which may increase anxiety. The desire to maintain the *status quo* is often a stronger impulse than the desire to solve a problem. Therefore, we must make a real effort to overcome the desire to keep the peace by being like others, and to avoid the innovative because it hasn't been done before.

It is argued that computers will eventually do most of our problem solving and decision making for us, and that we needn't bother to learn these skills ourselves. For these people, artificial intelligence (AI), which is at the cutting-edge of computer science, is proof of the triumph of machine intelligence over human intelligence. What too many of these dreamers forget, however, is that computers and their programs are designed and created by humans!

Author Stanford Beer, in his monograph "Managing Modern Complexity" wrote, "In the end when all the computers have crushed their numbers to the last intransigent bit, the unsquelched spirit of man takes the final responsibility for life or death."

Problem Solving Tip #6

The reason we fail to see the real problem is often due to sheer blindness. Sometimes the real problem is so hidden behind other problems, it becomes tangled up in its own ramifications or it's so hedged by technicalities that only patience, high intelligence, or special training can penetrate to it.

Howard Hodnett

Two excellent judges of AI achievements wrote books to drive home this reminder. The first was Joseph Weizenbaum, author of *Computer Power: From Judgment to Calculation* (1976); and the second was Sherry Turkle, author of *The Second Self: Computers and the Human Spirit* (1984). These authors, both academically and scientifically trained, re-emphasize the secondary value of so-called computer intelligence.

It's important to remember technology will dominate us only with our permission— if we believe it possible, and accept machines as equal or superior to human intelligence. Take a moment to consider how a computer could help you solve any of your present problems, and you'll see how short-sighted the notion of computer superiority is. Machine calculation or "intelligence" has its place, but it isn't at the forefront of human reason and judgment.

Problem-solving skills aren't developed automatically by weathering years of formal education or by being brought up by parents who stress classical thinking and logic. Outside the classroom and home we must practice our skills by solving adult problems. Problem solving requires the ability to think both clearly and creatively, and to judge, select and predict outcomes. Most importantly, it requires that we make decisions that bring about successful solutions. One problem-solving skill is knowing how to share our problems with others. The next chapter discusses how we can learn to do this.

SHARING PROBLEMS

*"Overwork among conscientious souls
is a far more real and frequent sin
than laziness."*

Evelyn Underhill

It's a relief to consider overwork sinful! Certainly, this supports all of the information we have heard in recent years about "workaholics." Most of us share our problems by talking about them to others, but we know little of how to truly and effectively share the burden of our everyday responsibilities. In business and other organizations, problem and task sharing have existed for quite some time. It is known as work or task delegation. There's no reason the same art of delegation can't be used in handling our everyday problems and responsibilities at home and work. If your major problem is overwork, as it is likely to be during the active years of adulthood, learning how to delegate will become an invaluable asset to you.

DISCOVERING THE BENEFITS OF SHARING

Although it may be easy to agree to the *idea* of delegation, many people find the reality of delegation to be difficult. In these times of two-paycheck families, children are increasingly involved in the responsibilities of household management and decisions out of necessity. Otherwise, parents would be obligated to pay someone else to perform these duties.

Many daily tasks are delegated to others when money is available, or when we don't have the time or expertise to do them ourselves. Even when we have time, we often delegate work because we have little interest in doing it, or would rather do something else. Economists call this kind of expense an *opportunity cost*, or a price we pay when the opportunity to do something else is worth the money.

A few benefits gained from successful delegation are time, money, and peace of mind. When you delegate a task, you can use the time to think or to formulate plans about other matters in your life, or you can earn additional money. Of course, with task delegation, the responsibility for the work remains with you.

Effective delegation involves sharing responsibility as well. At home, work, or in community organizations, you won't be relieved of your burden of duties until you can trust others to perform them competently. And this competence will never develop in members of your family, or in colleagues if they aren't given the opportunity to help you. Figure 4.1 shows how this delegation can be accomplished.

If you're overworked because you pride yourself on being a natural leader, or you take on additional duties regardless of your ability to perform them well, delegation is a solution you may want to try. You can retain the joy you find in leading a busy life by remembering that delegation involves *working* with others, while sharing the burden of responsibilities and tasks. You'll need to decide who can help you, and how you can prepare them to do so. Another aspect of delegation that will keep you mentally fit and challenged is learning to give up some control over the situation. For many of us, this is the *real* struggle. With delegation, we lose an element of control and power over situations. Many people find this threatening.

Figure 4.1
Delegation

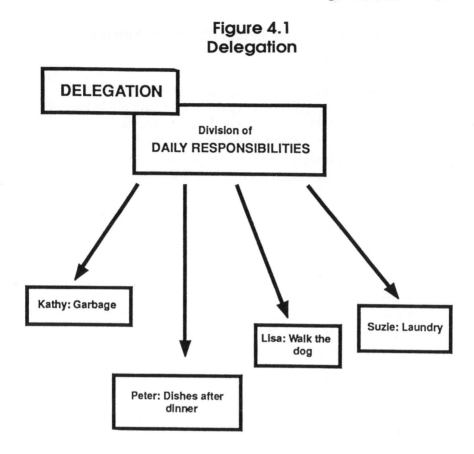

People who complain about problems to family members, friends, and coworkers often resist accepting solutions when they are offered. Many complainers never intend to solve their problems, because then they would have little to talk about! When complaining is a major part of any conversation, the exchange becomes tedious and repetitious. If you're serious about problem solving, and don't view the problems as topics for small talk and griping, delegation can work for you.

Although delegation sounds simple, in actuality it may be a difficult tool to use initially. We're often too set in doing things ourselves, and may have a hard time trusting others to do them as well. However, until we give others the opportunity and the experience of *cooperating with* us, rather than *working for* us, delegation remains only a possibility.

Problem Solving Tip #7

Don't be too quick to take back delegated authority. Making mistakes and
finding and correcting them is a useful
form of self-training.

Joseph J. Bannon

A manager who doesn't share and delegate effectively
becomes more of a worker than a manager. He or she works
harder, and yet produces less than a person who delegates
effectively.

CONFRONTING FAILURES IN SHARING

Below is a list of reasons why we fail in sharing responsibilities with others in our quest to become more effective problem
solvers:

* Lack of agreement about the work that is being delegated,
  particularly on the extent and scope of both parties' responsibilities, guidelines, or directions.

* Lack of assistance or training for those helping you.

* Lack of an understanding of your objectives.

* Your lack of confidence in those who are to help.

- Lack of confidence in your own ability to delegate, encourage, and motivate others to perform.

- Fear that others might outshine you.

- Fear from those who are helping you that failure will bring punishment or loss.

- Inability by all involved to see the value and benefits of delegation.

- Unwillingness to share or give up tasks you enjoy, or find easy to do.

- Expectation on your part for perfection.

- Belief that things are going well enough without change.

- Fear of taking any risks.

You may feel that you're too busy to even consider delegation. Just as with avoiding problems, avoiding delegation becomes a vicious cycle. We can get so bogged down with minor details and tasks that we're too busy or tired to see a way out. When this happens, we're often forced into a solution by ill health or some other crisis. When we fail to delegate in a timely manner, we neglect problem solving and give little thought to long-range plans, coordination of work, and preparing others to help share work.

Overworked people are not usually successful leaders, even though they deceive themselves into believing that ceaseless activity equals productivity. If you fit into this category, you may work harder, but have less to show for it than those who delegate effectively.

Problem Solving Tip #8

Be aware that delegation is a matter of self-discipline, and that achieving it will take time and practice.
                              Joseph J. Bannon

Too many managers aren't aware that delegation is a matter of self-discipline. Answer these questions to determine if you practice delegation.

• Do you always bring work home with you, from your job or other activities?

• Do you work longer hours than others with similar responsibilities and life styles?

• Do you spend much time doing for others what they can do themselves?

• Does work pile up for you if you're ill or gone?

• Are you still doing the same tasks you did before you got promoted, elected, or when your children were younger?

• Are you frequently interrupted or called upon for advice?

• Do you work out details that others could handle?

• Are you always rushing to make deadlines?

• Do you participate in too many activities, leaving little time for rest and recuperation?

If you answered most of these questions positively, you should seriously consider the benefits of delegation and take the time now to begin. Delegation encourages group responsibility and builds self-esteem and morale. These are qualities all of us could use more of in our jobs and at home.

UTILIZING THE AIDS TO SHARING

The following tips should help you take the first steps in delegating work among family members and other associates:

- Set realistic standards for what you seek to achieve and make sure everyone involved understands them. It's especially important to clarify these standards if you're cooperating with children and others unaccustomed to assuming responsibility.

- Understand that delegation is not a method for getting rid of work or for exploiting others. It's an ongoing process that encourages greater democracy in workplaces and in homes. Such participation is essential if you want to handle the pressures of home life and business competition.

- Choose the right person for the job. Delegation for its own sake is usually a mistake because care and consideration must be given to selecting and preparing the proper person to do a task. Know what others can do, or what they might be trained for, or encouraged to do.

- Decide what your objectives are for each delegated task. Discuss these objectives with those who are to help you, and make sure they have the resources to help effectively.

- If mistakes are made, make sure you correct others tactfully and privately.

- Reward those who do a good job, with money, praise, or more responsibility and authority.

- Be concerned and show interest in what others are doing to help you. This isn't an invitation to snoop. Active interest can spur others to greater achievement.

- Evaluate others' work on an ongoing basis so you both know if the objective is being achieved.

- If there are duties you want done to meet your standards of perfection, do them yourself as long as they don't represent the bulk of your work. Not all work should be delegated.

- Give further training to coworkers and associates if they require it or if they're moving toward greater responsibility.

- Don't take back work or responsibilities if mistakes have been made. Continue to encourage people to try again.

Figure 4.2 shows that delegation is appropriate in sharing family and home responsibilities as well as employment and career responsibilities.

Figure 4.2
Delegation worksheet

Tasks to be completed	Delegated to	Completion date desired	Cost parameter money-time	Training necessary
Letters	Office Assistant	August 6	100 hours	Business writing book
Mowing lawn	Son John	Tuesday of each week	3 hrs. per week. $15 per week	Safety tips about mower use
Plan July 4th special event	Club planning committee	June 1	40 hrs. Not to exceed $1,000	Purchase "Special Events Planning Guide"

Remember that to take advantage of delegation and to make it work for you, you must manage your own time well.

EXPLORING STYLES OF SHARING

Over the past several decades, there has been much discussion and research on different styles of management. The one you're probably most familiar with is top-down or authoritarian management, where one person at the top has ultimate responsibility. You may be less familiar with shared responsibility, or participatory management, in which bosses and workers, or family members try to share responsibility more equitably.

You may already have a style of leadership and wish to have a different style. Because of recent changes that have occurred in many families, presently less than ten percent of American families represent what has been referred to as the "ideal traditional family." Actually, one wonders if the ideal traditional family ever existed. In his book, *Maximum Life Span*, Roy Walford writes,

> "... popular belief in large multi-generation households of the past is illusory. Much less than 10 percent of all households in pre-industrial England contained more than two generations" (p.198).

Uncertainty and change in the home and the workplace force changes in how tasks get accomplished. For stability and some predictability, organizations and homes usually evolve a preferred style of completing tasks. However, there are situations in any organization or home that require different responses. For some matters, your style of problem solving or decision making may be more authoritarian than participatory. Your style or method shouldn't be inflexible, but you should select some agreed-on approaches to avoid chaos in the home or business.

As the pace of life and business quickens, the more authoritarian style of problem solving is disappearing, because it involves too much time. In *Future Shock*, Alvin Toffler observes:

"Bureaucracy, the very system that is supposed to crush us all under its weight, is itself groaning with change . . . we are witnessing not the triumph, but the breakdown of bureaucracy. We are, in fact, witnessing the arrival of a new (flexible) organizational system that will increasingly challenge and ultimately supplant bureaucracy" (p. 125).

Such flexible organizational styles have entered our homes, jobs and other associations. Some consider this breakdown of bureaucracy a breakdown in society and its values. If we accept one method of getting things accomplished as carved in stone, then, indeed, the upheavals and changes of these past few decades are threatening and very stressful.

But if we accept the inevitability of change, then the emergence of new problem-solving strategies can be considered a challenge instead of a threat. If you, your family, or organization are afraid of innovation and change, *any* new method of accomplishment will be frustrating. If you believe in sharing as a style of getting things done and solving problems, you should begin to try to do the following:

- Counsel, train, and help others to develop themselves;

- Communicate clearly and often with others;

- Tell others what is expected of them;

- Set high and clear performance standards;

- Learn your group or family's capabilities;

- Give others a fair share of decision-making discretion;

- Be aware of group or family morale, and try to keep it high;

- Keep others involved in the actual problem or situation, even when things aren't going well;

- Become willing to change how things are done; and

- Show your appreciation often, especially when someone does a good job.

To become successful at problem solving, you should also be willing to:

- **Cultivate flexibility,** shift roles as situations require;

- **Spend time planning,** daydreaming, offering help, or initiating the next step in any problem sequence;

- **Orchestrate the action** rather than direct the action;

- **Keep delegating the authority,** freeing yourself for other more important or relaxing options;

- **Support the decisions** of others to whom you delegate responsibility;

- **Develop loyalty** among group members;

- **Ask for and offer information** as needed, and encourage communication;

- **Give decision-making freedom** to others.

It should come as no surprise to you that not everyone is interested in sharing your problems. However, it might be surprising for you to learn that many people want more responsibility and freedom in decision making. Research indicates that the majority of American workers want more interesting and challenging work!

The important element in putting these desires to work for you is finding out what the people who live and work with you truly want before assuming your style of sharing responsibilities and rewards will be attractive to them. If you conclude they *are* interested in systematically solving problems together, the following chapter will introduce you to the steps involved.

5

UNDERSTANDING THE PROBLEM-SOLVING MODEL

*"The imagination is only free
when fear of error is temporarily
laid aside."*

Alvin Toffler

Although it is sometimes easy to point out that something is wrong, to assume the responsibility of correcting what is wrong requires thought and patience. Furthermore, sometimes problems are beyond our control. However, whenever you face a problem, you should begin to generate potential solutions for it. As mentioned in the previous chapter, many of us spend too much time complaining about problems. Successful problem solvers develop attitudes of *constructive* discontent to motivate themselves to find creative and workable solutions.

CATEGORIZING PROBLEMS

We must take the responsibility for solving our own problems. It is easy to blame others for the problems we face, and to point out faults in the system and other people; however, it is our responsibility to improve our own situation. Sometimes it helps to know if the problem you face has been solved before. If it has, you may be able to use a similar solution.

Problem Solving Tip #9

Find out if your problem has been solved before. If it has, find out if a similar solution will work for you.

Joseph J. Bannon

If the problem hasn't been solved before, it is still helpful to find out if anything is known about similar situations. With the exception of mechanical failure or equipment breakdown, no two problems are exactly alike. However, we can group problems with similar characteristics. Understanding these classifications will benefit you as you learn about and use the problem-solving method. The most common classifications are:

1. **Human relations problems,** which are caused primarily by the behavior of individuals or groups of people.

2. **Organizational and environmental problems**, which include difficulties related to procedure, policy, planning, budget and financial concerns.

3. **Technological problems,** which are caused by machine breakdown, computer problems, and electronic or system malfunction. (Technological problems can be difficult to solve, but they're probably the easiest to understand.)

Problem solving is unfortunately made more difficult by change and uncertainty. Too often the problems we face are poorly defined. Sometimes we discover that we're really dealing with more than one problem, or that the problem has multiple dimensions. The fact that 80 percent of new businesses fail, and that many people make only mediocre efforts at solving their problems points to the need we all have to develop our problem-solving skills.

UNDERSTANDING RATIONAL AND CREATIVE THINKING

Two methods of thought are central to the development of problem-solving skills: rational thinking and creative thinking. Rational thinking involves looking at problems in a systematic way. Creative thinking often appears to be a mere spontaneous flash of insight. So there seems, at first glance, to be a great difference between these two ways of thinking. However, what appears to be a spontaneous solution may actually be the result of years of experience and knowledge. We often try to compliment people who respond creatively to problems by telling them, "It's easy for you."

Such a compliment completely ignores why it seems easier for the person who's found *the* solution, or discovered *the* perfect way of doing something than it is for the rest of us to find the right answers. What appears to be a flash of insight is often the result of a very systematic approach to problems.

EXAMINING THE PROBLEM-SOLVING METHOD

If we draw a line between creative and systematic thinking, it should be a thin one. A good problem solver is both a systematic *and* a creative thinker. Experience, patience, and background all contribute to make an effective problem solver. In this book, you'll learn to approach problems with "systematic creativity." The model shown in Illustration 5.1 is a step-by-step approach to solving everyday problems.

Although we'll discuss this method in a step-by-step manner throughout the book, following a simple cookbook approach
won't always solve your problems. Some problems are more
complicated and uncertain than others because there may be
unexpected obstacles in the way. Also, don't forget that some
problems are simply unsolvable.

There may be aspects of a problem over which you'll have
little or no control. An example of an area that affords little room
for control is a situation in which one family member has a drug
or alcohol problem that blocks you from solving a smaller problem. It's nearly impossible to solve the smaller problem without
the larger one being removed.

For problems that *do* have solutions, however, following
these steps in the problem-solving model will improve your
ability to find solutions:

1. Define the problem situation.

2. Define the objectives of the solution.

3. Identify and observe any changes and conflicts that pre-
    vent achieving objectives.

4. Brainstorm for creative solutions.

5. Determine the pros and cons of several solutions.

6. Choose one "best" solution.

7. Develop a successful implementation strategy.

Figure 5.1
The Problem-Solving Model

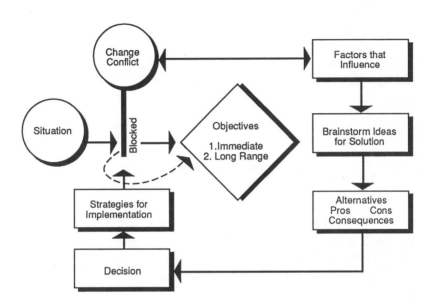

These seven steps needn't be slavishly followed, nor is one step always going to be clearly separate from the others. Steps may overlap, especially as you improve your problem-solving skills. The order in which I've presented these steps is based on personal experience, as well as the writings and experience of others. The steps will be developed in sequence throughout the book to make the problem-solving method easier to learn and follow.

Although it may be difficult to believe now, once you're familiar with their use, you'll be able to implement these steps very quickly. With practice, this recipe for action will become second nature to you — like riding a bicycle! Of course, the more complicated the problem, the more time each of these steps is likely to take. This is especially true when other people are involved. A leaky roof is easier to fix than a troubled relationship, or a complicated career problem.

The method, as shown in Figure 5.1, is a cycle or system. As we discuss it, I'll continue to provide examples of problems to help you visualize your own problems. You may also want to choose a problem of your own now and apply the problem-solving method steps to it as they're described. The first step in problem solving is defining the problem, and that's where we'll begin.

DEFINING THE PROBLEM

One of the best ways of identifying and defining the real problem is to ask the question: *Why?* If you ask this question about each of the symptoms of the problem you've encountered, you'll eventually uncover the real problem.

> ### Problem Solving Tip #10
>
> **Finding out the answer to the question "What is wrong?" is important, but it should be asked in the context of overall objectives, responsibilities, and practices.**
>
> **Richard I. Lyles**

Don't be satisfied with unclear or *I-don't-know-answers*. The problem-situation worksheet (Figure 5.2) will assist you in finding answers to questions important in arriving at a solution to your problem. You may want to take time now to fill out this sheet, using your own problem to answer each question.

Figure 5.2

My Problem-Situation Worksheet

What's going on in the problem situation?
_____
_____

What objectives do I want to accomplish?
_____
_____

What aspects of the problem situation can I control?
_____
_____

If the problem is not solved, what might happen?
_____
_____

Who is involved in the problem?
_____
_____

Where is the problem taking place?
_____
_____

What are possible reasons for the problem?
_____
_____
_____

We'll use this worksheet again in Chapter Six to narrow and clarify a concrete definition of your problem.

FOCUSING YOUR MENTAL ENERGY

The problem situation will be clearer to you when you focus your mental energy on the problem. By concentrating and narrowing your attention to the problem, you'll begin to find ways to solve it! It's been my experience that we don't solve problems for four basic reasons:

1.   *We have difficulty in defining the real problem.*

2.   *We haven't clearly defined our objectives.*

3.   *We don't develop a course of action to carry out our solutions.*

4.   *We decide it's just not worth the energy or time required.*

In the following chapters you'll learn to recognize factors that influence your problem, and obstacles that can hamper you; become familiar with brainstorming for solutions; discover how to select the best solution; and find out how to put the idea or solution you select into action. Again, in Chapter Six, we'll begin to implement the formal problem-solving method by further isolating and defining your problem.

6

DEFINING THE PROBLEM SITUATION

*"Eagerness to solve a problem or
to punch somebody in the nose—
before the problem has been
properly identified—accounts for much
of the inefficiency and grief associated
with the vast human activity of problem solving."*

Edward Hodnett

"*Something's wrong*" is the simplest definition of a problem. A problem exists when we sense a departure from a desired state of affairs. Certainly, a leaky roof is a shift from how we'd like things to be! A problem is most *obvious* when we're concerned enough to want to do something about it. In fact, it's probably at its worst when we're able to recognize it, or finally willing to admit that it exists. At this stage, we may be temporarily overwhelmed by its complexity.

However, once we earnestly begin the process of problem solving, a tempo will develop, encouraging us to continue. After we've solved certain types of problems, it's easier to solve similar problems. Gaining experience in solving problems will increase the speed with which we're able to find and implement solutions. In other words, the more we do to solve problems, the better we'll get, and the faster we'll be.

ZEROING IN ON THE PROBLEM

It's important to know that what seems, at first glance, to be the problem may be deceptive. Although it is tempting to try to solve problems quickly, taking time to distinguish the symptoms from the problem will ultimately save time and other resources.

As discussed in Chapter Two, the employees at the garage door company probably saved a large sum of their company's capital by taking the time to look beyond the obvious symptoms of their problem. Of course, it is theoretically possible to describe a universe of symptoms without identifying a problem. For this reason, it is crucial to delineate a cut-off point to speculation, beyond which you'll begin to zero in on the problem.

Identifying and defining the problem is the first and most critical step of the problem-solving process. If you don't identify and define your problem accurately, your decisions and actions will be off-target as you try to complete the rest of the steps of the process. Although you may feel that such analysis will only slow you down, it is time well-spent. There is nothing more wasteful and time consuming than attacking the wrong problem. During the initial stages of the process, the "doer" in you must step aside and let the thinker take over.

You may have one problem, a series of related problems, or symptoms of more than one problem. By separating problems and symptoms you can begin to identify and define your real problem. If you eliminate symptoms instead of solving the real problem, you may gain a limited amount of time, and achieve a temporary or an *interim solution* to your problem. (Interim solutions are discussed in more detail later.)

By taking time to separate the problem from its symptoms, you can reduce confusion as you try to study the problem situation. By isolating the *key problem,* or the problem you want to zero in on, you can realize the relative importance or unimportance of most of the symptoms and related problems. Information surrounds each problem that is significant to the development of a solution. Most problems have obvious and obscure facts that can be gathered or discovered.

Being aware of the obscure, the obvious, the factual, and the assumed is critical to finding a successful solution. For example, how often have you implemented a solution, only to realize later that your solution would have been different had you taken the time to check the validity of your assumptions, and to gather more information?

The type of information required depends on the nature of the problem. Fact finding and information gathering require creative thinking. The following procedures will help you obtain information that will aid you in developing a preliminary problem statement.

1.   **List questions you have about your problem.** What information would you like to have that you don't already know? This list may contain irrelevant, as well as relevant questions.

2.   **For each question, list sources where answers might be obtained.** Sources can include coworkers, family members, friends, government agencies, consultants, and professional and technical personnel.

3.   **Contact your sources and record their answers and observations.** This information may suggest additional questions that you may want to find the answers to.

The information worksheet (Figure 6.1) will help you in clarifying the information necessary to solve your problem.

Figure 6.1

Information Worksheet

Your preliminary problem statement:

_____

_____

_____

What additional information do I need that will help define
my problem more clearly?

Information   Sources   Additional information
                                              that would be helpful,
                                              if it were available

The following checklist will assist you in determining whether the information you collect should be screened further, challenged, or accepted.

1.   *Does the information suggest a redefinition of your problem?*

2.   *Is the information valid for the problem under study?*

3.   *Is the information sufficiently current to be valid?*

4.   *Do various information items support each other, or are they in conflict?*

5.   *If the information is contrary to your initial perception, are conflicts resolved to your satisfaction?*

6.   *Is there information that you don't trust as being accurate or representative?*

7.   *Are there relationships or associations between information items that should be explored further?*

8.   *If information items appear to impose a constraint on potential solutions, have they been verified by more than one source?*

DETERMINING CLEAR OBJECTIVES

What are your objectives? What do you wish to achieve? You need to know what you want before you can take steps to get it. If a problem is a departure from a *preferred* situation, then you must have a standard in mind for what you *do* want. Your standards may be ones you can clearly state, or they may be muddled or obscure.

> ## Problem Solving Tip #11
>
> **State the standards you have for achiev-
> ing your objectives clearly so that you
> can share them with others.**
> ### Joseph J. Bannon

Recently I was conducting a workshop for a group of real estate sales personnel. At the beginning of the workshop, I asked participants to write on a piece of paper the dollar amount they wanted to make during the coming year. Each participant had a fixed amount he or she wanted to achieve, and each automatically established a set of short- and long-term objectives that would be necessary to reach that amount.

It was interesting to observe that once everyone identified his or her short- and long-term objectives, many changed their annual desired amount. These agents either didn't want to spend the energy and effort to achieve their stated objectives, or they didn't have the time to carry out the responsibilities to achieve the desired amount.

The responses of the real estate agents weren't surprising. It's one thing to establish objectives, but all objectives have an immediate impact on the problem situation as well as on the future. Our future circumstances are often as important to us as our immediate concerns. So although we may think hopefully about an objective that provides the promise of gratification, we must consider what effect it will have on our lives in the long run. Figure 6.2 clarifies this concept in greater detail.

We should try not to set unrealistic objectives. In fact, you can keep objectives as narrow and modest as you wish, as long as they solve your key problem. For example, if you wish to get a promotion or pay raise, there is no need to concern yourself with *future* guarantees of such increases. Often it's better to focus on what you want in the present and plan to act similarly in the future if a comparable situation develops, than it is to develop

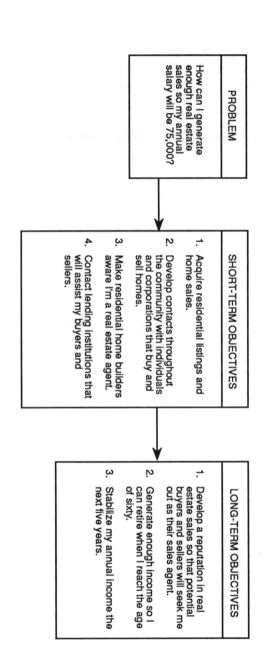

**Figure 6.2
Short- and Long-term Real Estate Objectives**

PROBLEM

How can I generate enough real estate sales so my annual salary will be 75,000?

SHORT-TERM OBJECTIVES

1. Acquire residential listings and home sales.

2. Develop contacts throughout the community with individuals and corporations that buy and sell homes.

3. Make residential home builders aware I'm a real estate agent.

4. Contact lending institutions that will assist my buyers and sellers.

LONG-TERM OBJECTIVES

1. Develop a reputation in real estate sales so that potential buyers and sellers will seek me out as their sales agent.

2. Generate enough income so I can retire when I reach the age of sixty.

3. Stabilize my annual income the next five years.

bold and elaborate objectives that may take much long-term planning.

Setting more modest goals may bring greater success than attempting too much. This isn't to say, however, that more elaborate and bolder objectives should be avoided completely. Chief executive officers of large companies have learned to think big as a way of life. Many now have contracts that include lucrative future objectives: If the company folds, they receive two to three years' salary, or if they're fired, they receive severance pay equal to this amount.

Certainly, there are rewards for thinking big, especially if you have the clout to get results. However, if you don't, or if you might jeopardize your goals by overextending the scope of your objectives, try to keep your objectives contained and modest.

CONSIDERING ALL VIEWPOINTS

As you zero in on your problem situation, in addition to deciding on what you wish to achieve, you must take into account the perspectives of everyone involved or affected by the problem and its solution. If you try to solve a problem using a perspective based solely on your or another person's desires, your efforts are bound to fail. No matter how well you think you know or could guess what another person's opinions and perspective might be, you should ask that person directly. Second-hand views are often inaccurate. Also, other perspectives can reduce the domination of your own biases or assumptions.

A close friend of mine was recently trying to make a decision as to whether he would accept a promotion with his company. This promotion would require a move to Seattle, Washington. On the surface, this seemed to be a great career opportunity. However, this decision would affect others who play important roles in his life. He recognized that if he made the decision without the input and support from those who were directly affected, he might create a disastrous situation for himself. Figure 6.3 details the considerations my friend faced.

Figure 6.3
The Seattle Scenario

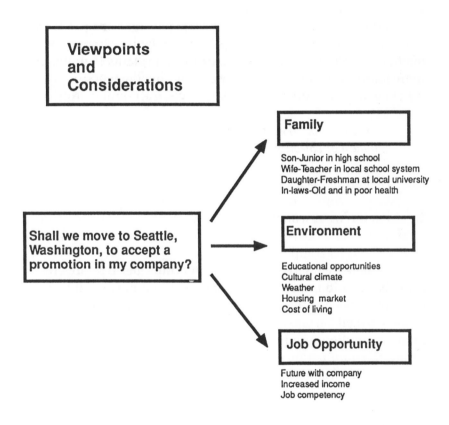

The decisions we make can affect many people around us. These people should be consulted, because if we fail to do this, we may find ourselves very much alone with limited or no support for the decision we make.

LISTING SYMPTOMS BY PRIORITY

When listing the various symptoms or signs of a problem, you should order them according to their *priority*. Although you may not recognize it at first, one of the symptoms is probably more important than all the others. To discover which symptom is the most important, you should ask yourself some questions:

1. *How much does the situation fall short of your standard or objective?*

2. *How serious is it?*

3. *What is the potential for improvement?*

That is— which of your problem symptoms, if removed or lessened, would improve the situation as you now see it? Furthermore, which of these symptoms, if eased or removed, would be most beneficial to all the other symptoms? To get the answers to these questions, you must ask more specific questions:

1. *How much difference is there between your desired objective and what exists?*

2. *Where is this occurring? (Location?)*

3. *When does it appear?*

4. *How large is it?*

5. *Who is affected by this difference?*

The question *Why?* isn't asked at this stage. You aren't trying to find the cause or source of the problem. You *are* narrowing the problem's definition. *Why?* will be an important question to ask when you've isolated the key problem and stated it clearly.

Writing a brief, clear problem statement can be amazingly difficult at first. Perhaps you've listened to other people trying to solve their problems and noticed that sometimes much of their discussion deals with side issues. This is rarely due to a reluctance to discuss the real problem. Often, they simply don't know what the real problem is! And, unfortunately, because they're muddled or confused, many of us get bored and lose our desire to help. At any rate, discovering the cause of a problem before clarifying the problem isn't possible.

WRITING DOWN THE PROBLEM

Now that you're familiar with the need to clarify and prioritize your objectives, seek others' viewpoints, and distinguish symptoms from problems, you're ready for the next step.

It is time to write down what you think your problem is. The earlier steps have helped you eliminate side or lesser issues, allowing you to concentrate on the key problem. Now try to state your problem as simply and briefly as you can. Because you may be sharing this statement with others, the clearer and briefer it is, the better for all concerned.

Problem Solving Tip #12

Define the problem so that you and others can generate possible solutions.
Joseph J. Bannon

It's essential that you state the problem in writing. As mentioned earlier, this is often difficult for many people to do. They can talk on and on about their problem, but when asked to reduce it to a few words, they're baffled. Writing makes a problem more tangible. You can "see" the problem, talk about it, and begin to solve it. Having a problem in writing keeps you focused.

You don't have to *keep* the problem stated in the same words that you originally chose. As you and others think and talk about the situation, the wording can be revised to be even more accurate and precise. Once you have written down a problem, (see Figure 6.3) it also becomes easier to separate it from its related symptoms.

Figure 6.3

PROBLEM SITUATION:

Write a statement about the problem
that concerns you most:

GATHERING HELPFUL INFORMATION

Next, you'll need to gather more information. You should put limits on the kind of information you want. Gathering all the facts, even if you have the resources, is almost impossible. Seek only information that is pertinent to your problem. The more useful your information, the better your chances are of solving your problem. As information is obtained, you may want to revise your problem statement. This means making your statement more precise and accurate. It does not mean changing the problem or discovering a new one.

Ignoring the need for information, or overlooking its relevance when it's obtained, won't benefit you as a problem solver. The quality and quantity of your facts often depend on the time and money available for information gathering.

Collecting facts can be tedious and time consuming. Don't spend time collecting irrelevant facts. Gathering information can be frustrating because many facts are simply not available. Make every effort to obtain all the facts, but don't be discouraged if these facts are not as precise or accurate as you would like them to be.

After gathering the facts, you must evaluate them to be sure you haven't allowed false assumptions or bias to creep in. Bias may be a difficulty throughout the problem-solving process, but it is most critical in the gathering and judging of information. Many facts are based on the assumption that things won't change, that they will remain the same into the foreseeable future. This assumption is risky because it is often wrong.

Try to anticipate the types of changes likely to occur in the information that you've gathered. The following chapters will discuss how to anticipate and deal with change.

7

DEFINING YOUR OBJECTIVES

"All progress stems from change, but all change is not necessarily progress."

1987 Farmer's Almanac

In Chapter Six, objectives were discussed to describe their fundamental characteristics and how those characteristics relate to the problem-solving process. Because these concepts are critical in learning how to define objectives, I will continue to explain their application to problem-solving situations.

Now that you have clarified your problem by putting it in writing, you need to decide exactly what you want to achieve in solving that problem. This step in the problem-solving process requires some careful thought. It is time well spent, however, because when thinking this way becomes a habit, you'll be able to solve future problems more easily.

You must find ways to evaluate the success or failure of your solution prior to implementing it. This kind of evaluation, or measurement, should be based on your objectives. As we discussed in Chapter Six, objectives can be either short or long term in scope, but you must determine their anticipated impact ahead of time.

FRAMING OBJECTIVES IN PRECISE LANGUAGE

Because objectives are so crucial to the process of evaluating your solution, they should be framed in precise and specific terms. They can't be vague or over generalized. Describing your objectives should never be put off until later. Procrastination at this phase of the process could cost you time and money later. For example, if you have a leaky roof, you want to know whether it is important to stop the leak for six months, twenty years, or for a single day. This knowledge will determine what you spend on the materials to fix it, how much time you'll be willing to invest in fixing it, and whether you need to consult experts to help you.

Problem Solving Tip #13

Responsible action is guided by clear-cut objectives. Effective problem solvers will constantly ask WHAT DO WE WANT TO ACHIEVE?

Joseph J. Bannon

Defining your objectives may not be easy. If you don't state your objectives precisely, you will find it harder to determine the most effective course of action than if you use words that can be understood, discussed, and, in some cases, even quantified. For example, if I say my objective is to improve my relationship with my daughter, I must ask myself what I mean by the word "improve," and in which area would I like to see this improvement occur?

If a student states that she would like to get an A in biology, she's stated a clear objective, but she hasn't described any meaningful method of how she might accomplish it, or how long she thinks she'll need to study to get an A, or even if she would like to get an A on one paper, for one semester, or in every biology course she ever takes.

Similar difficulties with imprecision and vagueness exist with admirable objectives, such as becoming an improved citizen, improving personal time management, and spending more time on charitable activities. Yet, with a little thought these ideals could be translated into specific objectives and shared with others. To move your objectives from the *"I-want-to"* stage to the accomplishment stage, you must state your objectives in precise language.

As well as stating objectives precisely, we must be careful to set objectives that are possible to reach. Never set an objective you suspect is impossible to achieve. Let's say our realtor friends in Chapter Six set an objective of $100,000 per year income, and accepted a workload compatible with generating that amount. Let's also say they suspect it's impossible to sell that much real estate in the present market. If it *is* impossible, they'll soon become frustrated. Eventually, they may suffer a total lack of motivation and wonder, "Why put any effort into something I'm failing to achieve?"

ESTIMATING THE NECESSARY RESOURCES

Economics is by far the most important factor in selecting realistic objectives. Before you start a project, try to determine just what resources you have on hand or can expect to muster in order to reach your objective(s). You may have determined, for instance, that your problem is the need to find another job, or to enter a new career field. Resources—primarily time and money— are themselves the means for obtaining or achieving this objective. These resources are essential to enable you to find or create another job.

If you have the resources and know what kind of job you want, your next step will be to determine how much lead time you'll need before you must have the new job. However, if your resources are limited, or if you simply want any job but the one you presently have, then your objectives will be more restricted. By stating your objectives in advance and mapping out what you'd like to achieve, you can avoid unexpected outcomes.

Unexpected outcomes are not always welcome surprises. It's better to think ahead to anticipate difficulties than to impulsively quit a job and hope for the best. In fact, taking the time to develop a clear set of objectives will probably ultimately determine how successful you are in solving any kind of problem.

CONSIDERING OTHERS IN YOUR OBJECTIVES

Some objectives are obvious, because they are part of your values or life style. You may know what you wish to achieve in the area of personal relationships or on a job because of instinctive guidelines or expectations that you operate within. These guidelines can serve as a framework for clarifying your objectives. For instance, in a family problem, your objectives might include bottom line values you won't compromise.

It is important to define broad-based objectives clearly and openly. Try not to hide anything from yourself or others that you consider an important objective. In other words, have *no hidden agendas*. This is especially important if anyone else is involved in the problem situation with you, or is likely to be affected by its outcome. Unwritten or hidden objectives, if they are important to a problem solution, must be examined. Denying or burying them solves nothing, and only makes problem solving more difficult than it needs to be.

Management expert Paul Mali pointed out that statements of objectives can't be structured and worded ignoring the fact that people of diverse backgrounds may be involved. Statements must relate in terms of how others feel and how they think. Ignoring the need to do this is to ignore the necessary two-way communication process.

In addition to revealing or clarifying your objectives, determine if these objectives are realistic. For instance, do they keep pace with, or reflect a situation as it actually is? You may wish a teenage son or daughter to behave in a specific and traditional manner. But if his or her friends or role models behave differently, or the expectations of adults toward young people are changing in the greater society, tradition-bound objectives may be unrealistic.

When confronting a challenge to your values as a parent, you may need to decide what you want to accomplish as a parent. How you handle a problem situation with your children may determine how they will behave in the future. I remember a number of years ago, when my oldest son announced, at age 15, that he was no longer going to attend religion classes on a weekly basis. My immediate reaction was, "You absolutely will."

Without thinking through the problem, I had established an objective of attendance. If I had remained insistent in achieving this objective, I would have created a confrontation between me and my son. As I pondered the situation, I reflected that my son was an outstanding student in school, well aware of right and wrong, aware of his responsibility to his peers, and well grounded in an acceptable set of ethical values. Had I maintained my initial objective of having him return to religion classes, I may have caused my future relationship with my son to change. By letting him make his own decision, I offered him the opportunity to grow socially and intellectually.

When we frame our objectives, we must be careful to avoid establishing what we want to achieve without giving full consideration to the consequences of doing so. Objectives should reflect what we wish to achieve, and what others involved in the problem want as well. Setting objectives isn't always an easy task, and it certainly isn't always done without controversy. If you or anyone else involved in a problem situation feels that traditional objectives are important, for example, then those objectives should be defended. Being traditional can serve you well if your aims are compatible with others who are affected by the situation, and if those aims are possible to achieve.

There is constant pressure for change in our society. It is far more important to understand the reasons for change, and decide what is important to uphold and what can be discarded. Those who cling blindly to past ways are often no better off than those who rush to greet every new fad or idea without much reflection.

Whether your objectives are traditional or untraditional, they must be clearly stated. Writing them down helps clear away confusion and vagueness in your thinking. If your problem is a sensitive one involving the feelings of others, any grievances they have must be aired.

There is no need to dream up objectives if what you want to achieve is clear or simple. If you're not sure what you want, or not confident you can attain what you want, then objectives are critical. Carefully examine what you already have achieved or accomplished with any solution you've already implemented before adding new objectives. Your list of objectives doesn't need to be final at this point in the problem-solving process. Objectives as well as problem statements can be revised as you move closer to solving your problem.

Problem Solving Tip #14

A statement of objectives cannot be structured and worded ignoring the fact that people of diverse backgrounds are involved. The statement must relate to those involved in terms of how they feel and what they think. To ignore this is to ignore the two-way communication that is necessary.

Paul Mali

Determine how long you would like a solution to last. Forever isn't possible or often desirable. Ask yourself whether you're seeking merely a stop-gap, or interim solution to your problem, or a more lasting one. You should consider and discuss your objectives in light of *intention, length, and flexibility*. One of the real estate agents might have written:

1.   I intend to become a real estate broker.
2.   I would like to remain in that field until retirement.
3.   I would settle for an early retirement, or become a real

estate salesperson, if the first two objectives are not possible.

By envisioning what you want and evaluating how you currently see your situation, you can begin to create meaningful future objectives. Your objectives needn't be arrived at logically. They can be stated as a result of personal or group brainstorming sessions. Brainstorming encourages us to temporarily let go of our logical, judgmental thinking processes. This process will be discussed in more detail in Chapter Nine.

Realistic objectives don't necessarily have to be traditional or modest. When you know what you wish to achieve, you can determine if it is possible, and if so, *how* it is possible. Beware of pitfalls, however. Some objectives are possible to achieve, but achieving them may jeopardize equally or more important goals. This is a liability of thinking big. If you grab for the brass ring, you may lose everything. An example of this kind of risk follows.

A divorced friend wished to finish her college education in order to become qualified for work in a profession that would allow her to support herself and her youngest son. Sarah (not her real name) was encouraged and supported in committing herself to this objective by all sorts of scholarships and loans that are made available for those with even a modest hope for success.

As it happens, she qualified for a wide array of scholarships and loans. Unfortunately, Sarah's objectives were vague. Because she formulated them almost out of a sense of desperation, she refused to even talk about them. Sarah simply wanted to improve her situation and get out of the rut of poverty that her divorce had created.

Unfortunately, Sarah's problems and the objectives she outlined for solving them had a strong relationship to time and money management. Yet, she felt so pressed by her desire to change her present life, she was disorganized and very shortsighted in her expenditures. Because her educational career and desire for a good job depended on the wise and careful allocation of limited resources, her inability to state distinct, specific objectives and evaluate her ability to reach them jeopardized everything.

Presently, Sarah is uncertain of completing her education and her student loans are due. Even the justification for continued scholarship help is doubtful. Her situation isn't simply a case of hardship. She was not fully prepared to think ahead. Most of us have made similar errors in judgment at some time during our lives. A full-steam-ahead attitude is not always a virtue when solving problems. The outcome in my friend's case may be the loss of even the little comfort and security she began with.

So you can see how objectives can be used as guidelines for problem solving. They provide a framework that distinguishes what is possible from what is not. Objectives can show us where we've been, where we're heading, as well as what we hope to achieve. They are check marks along a route that must be clearly and precisely mapped.

UNDERSTANDING VALUE AND FACTUAL OBJECTIVES

Many objectives you'll establish won't be *factual objectives*; rather they will be *value objectives*. Factual objectives can be measured or seen. Value objectives, on the other hand, must have a set of underlying qualities or beliefs that are agreed on by all who are involved with the problem and its solution.

It's possible sometimes to add facts and figures to value objectives, which makes them easier to describe, but for the most part, they are statements of quality rather than quantity, of philosophy rather than fact. There is no air-tight way of testing value objectives as we might test factual objectives. However, ethical consideration and commitment to values doesn't eliminate the need for facts. When you're faced with formulating a value objective, or handling an objective that has ethical and moral dimensions, beware of getting lost in philosophical discussions that do little to solve your problem!

No matter how broad and encompassing your objectives might be, they should add specificity to your problem statement without necessarily limiting its scope. In the case of my friend, Sarah, clear objectives — both value and factual — would have helped her move toward greater self-sufficiency without jeopardizing so much in the process. Her values of independence and self-determination may not have overridden the necessity for resources to support these values had she been able to more carefully frame her objectives.

Nothing occurs in a vacuum, not even our most idealistic aims. Compromise is important, if not essential, in solving most problems. As with all other aspects of problem solving, compromise should be determined by all persons involved with your problem and its solution. In most cases, you must be willing and able to compromise if you want to reach fair and constructive objectives.

EVALUATING OBJECTIVES AND SOLUTIONS

With your factual and value objectives as guidelines or checklists, you can begin to evaluate various solutions, retaining or discarding them depending how closely they meet your objectives. Perhaps my friend might have stated her initial objectives as follows:

1.   I wish to be financially self-sufficient and independent *(Combined Factual and Value Objective)*.
2.   I wish not to lose my home *(Factual Objective)*.
3.   I wish to obtain a college degree *(Factual Objective)*.
4.   I want the kind of lifestyle a better education may bring *(Value Objective)*.

Sarah focused on obtaining a degree at any cost, and as quickly as possible. In the short run, this solution threatened her rock-bottom goal of keeping her home. If she'd had the time and the emotional wherewithal to clarify her objectives (especially in terms of conflicts and contradictions), she might have revised her educational objective to one that would have allowed her more financial stability.

Writing objectives allows us to state what we would like to achieve, and to list the resources we would need to reach them. By listing the resources available to her, Sarah would have been able to recognize how her objectives were in basic conflict. Although she is admired by many for working so hard to fulfill a dream, she reports that those who are helping to pay her bills are somewhat less enthusiastic in their admiration. This illustrates again the importance of involving all those who are likely to be affected by an outcome.

After stating objectives in measurable terms, if they are factual, you should try to classify and rank them by importance. This step forces you to evaluate your objectives in relation to available or probable resources. Label the objectives *must* and *want*. The **must objectives** are those objectives that can't be violated by any solution to your problem. **Want objectives**, on the other hand, aren't as rigid, but reflect desired objectives.

Factual and value objectives can be either **must** or **want objectives**, depending on their importance to you and their likelihood of being reached. There is little point in fixing on **must objectives** that are unlikely to be met. You probably want to classify these as **want objectives** that have some chance of achievement, but they aren't objectives that you're willing to stake everything on to achieve.

You should list or chart these two types of objectives for review. It's amazing how clear many issues become when they are written down for all to see. You and others are much less likely to wander from the problem under discussion.

You can use the **must list** to discard any suggested solutions that do not meet these objectives. If you haven't spent time clarifying and distinguishing your objectives before this point, you may face the more disturbing task of having to discard or change your **must objectives** instead.

Your **want objectives** shouldn't be a dust bin for objectives you don't know how to classify. The **want list** shouldn't be a catch-all for lazy thinking. If some objectives don't fit either list, they are probably not critical to the immediate problem and should be discarded.

As you review your various objectives, you must anticipate the effect these objectives will have on the environment in which you live and work. Many difficulties you encounter will come from changes you weren't expecting in your environment when these objectives were set.

WRITING YOUR OBJECTIVES

Many management consultants and practitioners have suggested guidelines for formulating objectives. As you develop yours, you should check these guidelines to be consistent with these suggestions. All of them may not apply, but most will provide you with a basis for analyzing your written statements. I'm listing some here that may be helpful to you.

1. **Start with the word "to" followed by an "action" verb.** By doing so you'll establish a mind set of activity. Use words such as "to provide," "to establish, "to demonstrate," "to improve," "to develop." Using words such as these motivates you to a commitment of action.

2. **Specify a single key result to be accomplished.** At some point, you'll want to determine whether or not you accomplished your objective. Your objective statement should never state more than one result. More than one result clutters the clarity of your objective. By establishing one key result you will know when you get there.

3. **Specify a target date for its accomplishment.** By establishing a specific date for accomplishment you will minimize the possibility of procrastination. We all know it's easy to do it tomorrow. If we establish a target date for completion and do not meet the deadline, we develop a guilt complex. Of course there may be very good reasons for not meeting the established target date, but at least you will have some idea as to why the objective is not accomplished.

4. **Specify cost factors — both dollar and people costs — that will be required to achieve your objective.** Almost every objective you establish will have cost factors that will be unaccounted for if they aren't given serious thought in the very beginning. It's been my experience in working with individuals in my workshops that these considerations are often forgotten and not given appropriate concern. If you fail to consider your costs, chaos is guaranteed to result.

5.   **Be as specific and quantitative as possible.** It is clearer to state, "I will spend each Sunday afternoon with my daughter in a recreation activity," than it is to state, "I will spend more time with my daughter."

6.   **Specify the "what and when" and "why and how".** As mentioned previously, describe what you want to accomplish and a time line for completion. If you attempt to describe the justification and the procedure you'll use to accomplish it, a clash will occur. A different thought process takes place in these two strategies. If you try justifying increasing funding for your agency at the same time you attempt to establish procedures for generating funds, you will inhibit and retard your thought process.

7.   **It should be clear and understandable to those who will be responsible for carrying out the objective.** As a problem solver you'll quickly learn that it will be impossible to execute solutions if you don't have the support from those who must carry them out. Obviously you can't do all the tasks yourself. You will need to make assignments to others. If you expect subordinates or personal contacts to successfully carry out their tasks, the objectives should be very clear. If they aren't, then opportunities for discussion and clarification should exist.

8.   **Your objectives should be achievable and attainable.** Don't establish objectives that are impossible to achieve. Make sure the individuals who will assist in your problem-solving effort are competent and that resources are available to accomplish the objective. If you don't, you're setting yourself up for failure. If an objective is clearly unattainable, it will soon be recognized as such. If this happens, frustration and demotivation will set in.

9.   **Be consistent with the mission and goals of the overall problem solution.** Every task you carry out should have a relationship to the overall mission or you shouldn't be doing it. You should examine this relationship frequently.

I often observe individuals engaged in tasks that have little or no relationship to their ultimate goal.

10.   **Objectives should be put into writing.** Carry them on note cards, and look at them frequently. Constantly remind yourself of what you're trying to accomplish. Reading your objectives in print can motivate you to act. It also eliminates confusion.

When objectives are stated in writing, everyone involved in the problem-solving process will know what you're trying to accomplish. Any list of what you wish the problem solution to achieve doesn't need to be final at this point. Objectives, as with the problem statement itself, can be modified as you move closer to solving your problem. In the next chapter, we'll examine factors that can influence problem solving.

IDENTIFYING FACTORS INFLUENCING CHANGE AND CONFLICT

*"The first step in solving your
problems is taking responsibility for them.
It's very easy to blame others for
problems that you face. It is easy
to point out faults in the system and in
other people, it's quite another thing
to take responsibility to try to make things better."*

William P. Anthony

There are many factors that influence our problems and the solutions we consider. In addition to becoming familiar with these factors, you'll need to recognize which of them are the most critical to you. Through a process of elimination and good judgment, you can learn to isolate the factors that require your attention.

EXPLORING CHANGE

The most important factor in any problem we face is *change*. If you have read Alvin Toffler's *The Third Wave*, you're familiar with the negative and positive forces of change in all of our lives. According to Toffler, change is unavoidable, and it is also growing more complex, and occurring at a faster rate as we move toward the next century.

In the last two years, we've witnessed major changes in the national and international scenes. Who would have predicted the United States would have 500,000 troops in Saudi Arabia; communism would collapse in Eastern Europe; the reunification of Germany would occur; Nelson Mandela would be released from prison; the Soviet Communist Party would be banned, and a Japanese company would be the sole owner of MCA, a major U. S. entertainment industry?

Change can be either simple or complex, unusual or routine, and negative or positive. In its simplest form, change is a modification of anything in our environment. Your problem may be the result of change, either simple or complicated, unplanned or intentional, bizarre or unanticipated.

We're usually more concerned about negative rather than positive change, but there are exceptions to this rule. A positive change, such as inheriting money or getting a promotion, can pose as many problems as more negative changes. Of course, these changes are more exciting to deal with because they expand our possibilities. Negative change, on the other hand, usually limits and restricts our actions, while costing us time and money. You may want to focus on the changes that relate to the problem that you are dealing with now.

As you concentrate on the impact of change on your problem, consider these two aspects: whether the change is negative or positive, and how long it's likely to last. In addition, review *what* has changed and reflect on *why* it has changed. You may be surprised to note over time that the major change you uncover is almost always the cause of your problem. The following example shows how one change can affect several industries.

In the mid 1970s, there was a significant decline in attendance at national parks. Numerous factors influenced this decline. One of the more important changes was the increase in gasoline prices from about 35¢ per gallon to $1.00 per gallon. Prior to 1975, travel expenditure to and from the national parks was of little concern to individuals and families who wanted to vacation in them. However, when the price of gas tripled, travel expense became an important factor in deciding whether to vacation at a national park, and park attendance declined.

The increase in petroleum cost during this period also caused a slump in the recreation vehicle (RV) industry because RV's only get about five to eight miles per gallon of gas. Consumers naturally had second thoughts about whether buying an RV was a wise expenditure of their recreation dollar. The Winnebago Company, one of the largest manufacturers of RV's, encountered serious money difficulties during this time period.

To identify the cause of a problem, we need to separate the major change from other less important changes. Earlier, we concentrated on identifying and defining the problem. Now, we must concentrate on isolating its *cause* before we can consider its possible solutions.

Because solutions are directly related to a problem's cause, we must zero in on any changes that are directly related to the problem. One of these changes is probably the key cause. We didn't concentrate on finding the problem's cause earlier because when we compare the changes in our environment with a well-defined problem statement, it becomes easier to discard those that have no apparent connection.

Problem Solving Tip #15

To deal with change effectively, get the right people with the right attributes into the right roles at the right time.
                                    Joseph J. Bannon

A few examples of areas we have become accustomed to seeing affected by change include financial, emotional, psychological, political, climatological, technological, generational, sociological, and international. Changes in these areas, as well as others, may or may not affect your specific problem.

The cause of your problem may be no mystery, or it may be very subtle. Ideas about what changes have taken place in your problem situation had probably occurred to you as you moved through the problem-solving process. You can now bring them forward and review them. However, try to consider only the obvious and truly possible causes at this point. Avoid being sidetracked on tangents about cause and effect. Remember—this isn't a philosophical exercise! It's an attempt to solve your everyday problem.

Problem Statement: No money for dental check-up

Possible causes:

1.   Spent $30 on entertainment

2.   Insurance payment due

3.   Rent went up

4.

5.

As you review the changes that are likely to be the cause, put them in order of priority based on which is the more probable cause. Remember to review only those changes that are obviously related to your problem. The number of changes will generally be small, so your review won't be time consuming. The causes you find can be tested by comparing their relationships to the problem.

When you've reviewed, compared, and tested the causes, you can write a *change statement*. As clearly and briefly as possible, state what change or changes you believe caused your problem. If you need more information on any of the changes, take time to gather your facts. As mentioned, fact finding and information gathering occur throughout the problem-solving process.

Once you've isolated, identified, and written down what you believe is the change that caused your problem, you can begin to consider various solutions. Any solution itself involves change. Few problems are solved by doing nothing. However, resistance to change is common, and this is a major barrier to solving problems. Eric Hoffer, in his book, *The Ordeal of Change*, in 1962 wrote:

> "It is my impression that no one really likes the new . . . Even in slight things the experience of the new is rarely without some stirring of foreboding" (p.1).

The denial of change, as Alvin Toffler discusses it, is disbelief in possibility. Such disbelief is represented by Albert Einstein's statement in 1932:

> "There is not the slightest indication that nuclear energy will ever be obtainable. It would mean that the atom would have to be shattered at will."

That is, of course, precisely what happened. There are many equally impressive examples of denials of the possibility of change by experts who sometimes are the very ones to prove themselves wrong.

Disbelief in the possibilities of telegraphs, automobiles, airplanes, atomic and nuclear energy, television, or space flight came from generations not as familiar with rapid technological and cultural changes as we are today. In fact, today we may run the opposite risk, believing that anything is possible, that rapid and frequent change is always for the better, and that change cannot and should not be forestalled. Toffler wrote of the "high" we can experience by making healthy adjustments during rapid and frequent change:

> "The 'new' society that is evolving in the industrialized West offers the supreme exhilaration of riding change, cresting it, changing and growing with it . . . It presents the individual with a contest that requires self-mastery and high intelligence. For the individual who comes armed with these, and who makes the necessary effort to understand the fast-emerging, super-industrial social structure, for the person who finds the 'right' life pace, the 'right' sequence of subcults to join and life style models to emulate, the triumph is exquisite."

While the exquisiteness of such a super-human life style and pace can be questioned, it's important to acknowledge that change itself may be more attractive, unavoidable, and necessary than ever before in recorded history — a change in itself!

As I've conducted workshops on problem solving over the past 30 years, I've heard much resistance to change, including statements such as:

- We have never done this before.
- We've done this before and it didn't help.
- This is against a policy or tradition.
- This won't work because . . .
- My kids or mate won't like this.
- This community is not ready for this.
- My boss is against this.
- This costs too much.
- This is too time consuming.
- This might work elsewhere, but not here.

You can probably come up with more objections from your own experience. We all need to remember that no matter how appealing and nostalgic tradition is, it must be kept at a minimum in problem solving. Hearing for the hundredth time, "We've never done it that way before," is tiresome and energy draining.

Perhaps unfortunately, most of us are nearer to Eric Hoffer's than Alvin Toffler's description of response to change. Most of us are more comfortable with familiar situations. We tend to resist change, no matter how minor because the unknown and untried can be threatening. No matter how much a change may benefit those involved in your problem, *never* assume it will be automatically and joyfully accepted.

The risks we perceive as being inherent in change are related to the type of change involved. There are routine changes and more radical or serious changes. Routine changes may cause little difficulty or adjustment. These include changes in procedures, habits, roles, finances, or other daily activities and expectations. Radical changes, on the other hand, are significant changes including family composition, organizational changes at work, regional or international relocation, and rapid changes in lifestyle. Examples of such changes are a wife returning to work, the death of a family member, and so-called acts of God.

Open, flexible attitudes can foster the ideal atmosphere for solving problems. In reality, however, our attitudes toward change may never quite mirror Toffler's adaptive "high" but they can certainly be less rigid than Hoffer's description of reaction to change. A responsive, realistic, and balanced attitude toward change can help us avoid many problem-solving barriers.

LIVING WITH CHANGE

Other attitudes may pose serious blocks to problem solving. Although we can assume that everyone involved in the problem agrees on the need to solve it, we can't assume everyone will agree on one solution. This lack of agreement is a common and serious barrier. We must work and communicate closely with everyone involved or affected by a problem throughout the process.

This is especially true when the problem involves conflicts of values or expectations. Any assumptions about preferred solutions will probably meet a sad fate. Even accurate information about the changes that a solution may make in the problem situation, won't clear all obstacles from our paths. You can probably come up with recent examples of this situation in your own experience. To reduce resistance to change, avoid vagueness about it throughout the problem-solving process.

Problem Solving Tip #16

Learn to meet change by being open and flexible in your expectation of your abilities and the abilities of others, as well as in the inevitability of change.
                                    Joseph J. Bannon

How we see things—our perception of reality—involves not only how we actually view things, but how we intellectually and emotionally interpret them. Everything we see or perceive is filtered through a prism of preconceptions and expectations. Faulty perceptions can be the result of poor childhood training or education, or of clinging to outdated or inflexible values and habits.

As we discussed previously, being flexible doesn't mean we must bend with every breeze, but that we modify our behavior and attitudes in terms of an ever-changing reality. Faulty perceptions become obvious when someone is presented with new or challenging information and he or she jumps to an outdated conclusion. Perceptual blocks are also evident when we're unable to transfer experience from one aspect of our lives to another. One premise of this book is that what you learn here about a particular problem can easily be applied to other problem situations.

As we observed previously, cultural and ethnic blocks can seriously impair problem-solving abilities. If prejudices against African Americans, women, untraditional young people, or anyone else are part of your heritage, you've got a lot to overcome. Some people conform to such beliefs in order to be accepted by one group. When they shift to another group or situation, such prejudices can seriously hamper them, especially if they remain unspoken or assumed.

Group or family pressures may lead us to conform to an entire range of questionable behaviors. Sexual and racial prejudices are so widespread that some of us could spend a lifetime not encountering much opposition to them. As we've noted, such attitudes will only cripple our ability to work and achieve with people we're unfamiliar with or who we fear.

It is worth emphasizing that narrow values can exist on the job. Co-workers may not wish to exert themselves beyond a certain limit, which is usually only what safeguards their positions. Cultural blocks may cause associates to frown on anyone more ambitious than they are because the group is content with a low-level status quo. Unless we're aware of such unadmitted assumptions, we might conform in order to be accepted by the group. If you come across this situation and you're independent, you may choose your own level or style of activity, or you may decide to find another work environment.

No doubt the greatest emotional block in problem solving is fear. If we're afraid to set important or innovative objectives, or are afraid of the consequences of any solutions, our skills as problem solvers will be seriously impaired. Fear may exist because we don't know enough about a problem to attempt a solution, or because we're anxious about making decisions, and prefer to leave them undecided.

There's nothing wrong with having emotional reactions to problem solving. In fact, it's quite normal and healthy. However, remember to be aware of your emotions, especially if they prevent you from finding solutions to your problems. Again, several of the more common blocks to problem solving are:

Habits. Solving problems often means doing things differently. The way things are currently done may be comfortable, a habit difficult to break. Often there is little awareness of habits and how they affect problem solving.

Perceptions. Perceptions affect how problems and solutions are seen. Developing the ability to see things from different perspectives, or from another's viewpoint can help us overcome short-sightedness.

Fears. Everyone has fears. Sometimes effective problem solving is blocked by our unrealistic fears, those that exist in the mind rather than in reality. Some of these fears include fear of failure, fear of being laughed at, or fear of rejection.

Assumptions. Assumptions are often accepted in place of facts. Assumptions may be made about what the problem is or is not, what solutions are possible or impossible, and whether an attempt should even be made to solve the problem.

History. A too-beloved knowledge of what has happened before, what solutions have been tried, and what has and has not worked will lead to making assumptions and to being comfortable with the status quo.

Change. Problem solving implies changing something that exists to something new. Change is difficult for everyone. Resistance to change in some form is a natural reaction. When all the other blocks are overcome, this one will still have to be dealt with.

As you attempt to control the blocks that prevent problem solving, you should realize that a change in your values doesn't necessarily lead to a change in your behavior, or vice versa. You may accept the need for a change, yet be unable to eliminate the various blocks to making that change.

If we were solving problems in a social vacuum, we would only have to consider our own blocks to a problem. However, most of us work with others and have to anticipate their blocks as well as our own. As we anticipate such blocks, we should be realistic about the blocks or barriers that we can influence and those we can't. Not all blocks can be removed or avoided. We may be able to offset ignorance and resistance to change by encouraging others to see the value and appeal of new ideas and viewpoints. But, for now, let's turn to the next chapter and to searching for solutions to your problem.

9

BRAINSTORMING FOR CREATIVE SOLUTIONS

"Creativity has its own form of immortality, for an idea placed in civilization may grow for hundreds of years, bringing a different existence to unborn generations."

Robert Crawford

Creative thinking isn't a gift or talent that's necessarily limited to a small number of people. It can, to some degree, be learned. Our intellectual and creative capacities may actually expand with "exercise." This exercise should include daily decision making and problem solving.

DEFINING CREATIVE THINKING

Creative thinking, the process of trying to come up with new and innovative ideas, is extremely valuable and necessary for effective problem solving. This is especially true when we encounter new types of problems, or when old solutions no longer seem to work. Creativity doesn't simply mean coming up with way-out solutions to simple, everyday problems. It really means learning to think broadly and inventively about problems that don't have quick, easy solutions. Creativity involves taking the time to:

- *Shift the style and tempo of our thinking;*

- *Break with old habits of thoughts; and*

- *Encourage other modes of thinking to emerge.*

Most of us can be trained and encouraged to use our imaginations more effectively. This chapter focuses on one creative method —brainstorming — to stimulate people to become more creative in their thinking.

Four Methods of Thought

Using only one method of thinking can be a barrier to developing your abilities in other methods of thought. For example, you may deny yourself the rewards of creative thinking, if you trust only logical thought processes.

Problem Solving Tip # 17

Brainstorming is not a method to solve problems, but is a technique for generating ideas that are potential solutions to problems.

Joseph J. Bannon

Basically, we think or order information in four ways: analytically, judicially, politically, and creatively.

Analytical thinking involves pure or applied logic, such as in mathematics, systems analysis, operations research, and especially computer programming.

Judicial thinking involves laws, rules, regulations, and policies with which we're familiar and to which we conform.

Political thinking includes behavior we've developed to get things done without getting side-tracked by logic or law. Political thinking involves maneuvering, compromise, planning, and influence.

Creative thinking is more open than the other three methods of thinking. It involves suspending judgment of ideas, speculating and exploring, daydreaming, moving from the apparently irrelevant to the relevant, and welcoming and encouraging purely serendipitous ideas as they pop up.

Figure 9.1 encapsulates the characteristics of each of the four methods of thought just presented.

Figure 9.1
The Four Methods of Thought

WAYS WE THINK

ANALYTICAL	JUDICIAL	POLITICAL	CREATIVE
Pure Logic	Law	Bureaucratic	Organized Mind Wandering
•mathematics •systems analysis •operations research	•rules & regulations •policies •acceptance	•maneuvering •compromise •planning •influence	•suspend judgment •serendipity •exploration •dreaming •irrelevant to relevant

Personal Traits and Creativity

Many believe taking advantage of better nutrition and planned exercise can enhance our mental abilities and skills. Personal computers, with their vast array of increasingly fast and complex programs, can enhance our knowledge and abilities. However, we don't have to rely only on diet, exercise, and computers to stimulate creative thinking.

In the last few decades much research has been conducted to discover how less creative people can be made to think and act more creatively. At one time, the popular image of a creative person was someone who was a loner, a person who seemed separate even when working with others. This image has become less prevalent as the pace of change has quickened.

In order to gather ideas, insights and stimulation, a creative person today is likely to be involved with many different kinds of people and groups. The loner image is less commonly descriptive of current inventors, artists, and thinkers. Most inventions and innovations from science, industry, and even, to some degree, the arts are coming from groups and organizations.

Researcher J.P. Guilford describes the characteristics of creative people. You may want to think of people you consider to be creative and see where these characteristics match their personality traits and where they don't.

PERSONALITY TRAITS OF A CREATIVE INDIVIDUAL

In relation to others, a creative person:

- is not a joiner
- has few close friends
- is independent of parents, peers, community
- is usually dominant
- is assertive, bold, courageous
- has little interest in interpersonal relations

- displays independent thought, even when pressured
- hews to a conventional morality

In job attitudes, a creative person

- prefers things and ideas to people
- has high regard for intellectual interests
- places less emphasis on job security
- finds little joy in detail work and routine
- is resourceful and adaptable
- is skeptical
- is precise and critical
- is honest and demonstrates integrity
- can toy with elements, is able to be puzzled
- has a high tolerance for ambiguity
- is persistent
- places emphasis on theoretical values

In attitudes toward self, a creative person

- is introspective and egocentric
- displays openness to new experiences
- has less need to protect self
- has a great awareness of self
- has attained inner maturity
- has great eye strength
- demonstrates strength of character
- is highly responsive emotionally
- is less emotionally stable than most others
- has less self-acceptance than most others

More characteristics of a creative person are

- spontaneity, enthusiasm
- stubbornness
- originality
- adventurousness
- high excitability and irritability

- compulsivity
- impulsivity
- complexity as a person
- anxiety

I like to describe creative thinking as an organized mind "wandering." Unfortunately, when we daydream and let our thoughts wander, we're too often criticized for wasting time. In fact, for many of us, letting go enough to let our thoughts wander is quite difficult. We have too many barriers against the kind of relaxed attitude and lack of judgment such thinking requires.

This is especially true if we've been trained in logic. To logical thinkers, a wandering mind may seem to be a troubled mind. In fact, the word "brainstorm" was originally used to describe the "diseased condition" of a deranged mind. Perhaps this is why many people are afraid of being more creative and may resent creativity in others.

BRAINSTORMING TO STIMULATE CREATIVITY

Brainstorming is a relatively simple procedure. It amounts to a group of people tossing out ideas as fast as they can be recorded without outside or self-criticism. There is no discussion, elaboration, or selling of any particular idea. When the exchange of ideas slows, a moderator tries to restimulate the group. Participants listen to each other to improve, modify, and combine their ideas to increase the number of alternative plans. When the time limit is up or an arbitrary quota of ideas has been generated, the moderator closes the session by thanking the group and requesting that any after-session ideas be recorded and sent immediately to him or her for inclusion in a typed list. The session should be relaxed, informal, and friendly.

Brainstorming is a creative technique for problem solving that encourages us to think up radically new ideas and techniques. It doesn't initially require that we combine good judgment with good ideas. We're actually encouraged to ransack our brains for ideas. Ideas are stimulated to come from the reservoirs of our subconscious minds where, as we discussed in Chapter of our subconscious minds where, as we discussed in Chapter Three, most creativity and inspiration is believed to originate. These thoughts and ideas can begin a chain reaction, or storm, of other ideas in a process of free association.

Most of the ideas may be silly, crazy, or impossible, but as Alvin Toffler wrote in *Future Shock*:

> "The essence of creativity is a willingness to play the fool, to toy with the absurd, only later submitting the stream of ideas to harsh critical judgment."

When brainstorming for solutions, everyone is encouraged to think in a free-ranging manner, and to offer as many ideas and suggestions for solving the problem as possible. There should be no criticism during a brainstorming session. Unusual perspectives, innovative solutions, and wild shots should be encouraged. Participating in brainstorming should be stimulating and exciting. The tempo of exchange is often finger-snapping fast.

As ideas come up, participants build on them, adding their own ideas and suggestions to those of others. If you're brainstorming alone — giving yourself permission to think without censoring yourself with "good judgment" — feel free to travel down paths of thought that you can change at will. Success in problem solving means nurturing, to some degree, apparently irrelevant ideas that may actually be useful for a particular problem.

Brainstorming may appear to be a substitute for more logical approaches to problem solving. It seems, at first glance, to demand little training or discipline, to be nothing more than an unplanned bull session. Nothing could be further from the truth. Brainstorming can be crucial to problem solving, a creative ingredient of more traditional styles of problem solving. Although brainstorming in itself isn't a way to solve problems, it is a way to generate potential solutions.

By withholding our judgment, we can generate a broader array of ideas than if we censor our thoughts. Waiting to evaluate and assess is called *deferring judgment,* and it's the key to successful brainstorming. Often, we're under pressure to be creative and practical at the same time. These two ways of thinking are incompatible and interfere with each other. The cold eye of judgment a brainstorming ground rule, you'll have many more ideas to choose from for a solution. You may look critically at the ideas later, perhaps a day or so after brainstorming.

DISCOVERING THE BENEFITS OF PERSONAL BRAINSTORMING

If you've labored over a problem without finding a satisfactory solution, you've probably become frustrated. Writers, artists, composers, and scientists sometimes feel "blocked" on a problem. They're unable to see it in a fresh and meaningful way. The best thing to do when this happens to you is to get away from the problem and, as some suggest, sleep on it or let it incubate.

The incubation of ideas has its advantages. It provides your mind with a change of pace, and may provide new light to your search for a solution. Also, incubation gives ideas for solutions time to "grow." Perhaps in the course of several days or weeks, what began as a germ of an idea will develop into a full-fledged idea with the viable potential of solving your problem. Another advantage of deliberately harnessing your subconscious—which is what incubation is all about — is that it greatly increases your mental energy.

Among the people who believed in the power to incubate deliberately were the composers Horfmann, Paderewski, and Kreisler. These men made it a practice to spend hours in idle thinking. Charles Tellier, the French engineer, claimed that his greatest discoveries were made in the course of quiet strolls while his mind was busy enjoying the peaceful scenery. One observer reported that John Jacob Astor's most striking characteristic was the patience with which he would wait for one idea to "come into full flower."

Sir Isaac Newton was another scientist who believed in thinking continually by harnessing his subconscious, as did John Von Neumann. Von Neumann reportedly believed that pure concentration alone was never enough to solve difficult mathematical problems and that these were solved in the subconscious. He frequently went to bed with an unsolved problem and woke in the morning to scribble the answer on a pad he kept on the bedside table.

Incubation has often been referred to as "sleeping on a problem." In business and dealing with personal problems, the time you have to incubate a particular solution may be the time you can readily make in the course of the day. It may mean breaking away from your desk for a walk, leaving the house for a short time, or taking a coffee break. Or it may mean timing your activity on a problem so that you can mentally lay it aside while you go to lunch.

It's helpful when you can wait overnight, or take a two- or three-day break to let your subconscious take over the problem. If you can allow yourself the time, take it. However, don't let incubation become an excuse for procrastination. You can polish, refine, and improve on an idea so much that the original spark is extinguished. Give yourself enough time to incubate an idea, but not enough to smother it!

ESTABLISHING A BRAINSTORMING GROUP

Although you can brainstorm alone, engaging a group of friends, coworkers, or others who are involved in or interested in your problem may really help. Brainstorming has been criticized for denying an individual's ability to solve problems by stressing reliance on a group. However, rather than denying individual thought, brainstorming acts to stimulate thought.

Problem Solving Tip #18

Brainstorming is a workable way of jointly producing more and better ideas than is possible through the usual type of conference in which judicial judgment jams creative imagination.

Alex F. Osborn

In terms of time and energy, more than one person brainstorming is very productive. Research shows improvement in both individual and group problem-solving skills when brainstorming is used. If you have already set up a traditional family meeting or work conference, you can substantially improve the productivity of your group with training in brainstorming. For family and other personal matters, "heart-storming," which is a method to encourage the expression of feelings, emotions, and desires is also appropriate.

A few basic rules

First, it's important not to lose sight of your problem. Put the written problem statement (as formulated in Chapter Six) in a conspicuous place so the group can see it at all times. This will help everyone focus on your ultimate goal.

Second, make sure that everyone understands and follows some formulation of these four basic rules developed by Dr. Alex Osborn:

1.   **Criticism is ruled out.** Judgment is suspended until subsequent evaluation.

2.   **Freewheeling is welcomed.** The wilder the ideas, the better; it is easier to tame down than to think up.

3.   **Quantity is wanted.** The greater the number of ideas, the more the likelihood of good ones.

4.   **Combination and improvement are sought.** In addition to contributing ideas of their own, panel members should think how suggestions of others could be turned into better ideas, or how two or more ideas could be combined into a still better idea. Hitchhike on others' ideas.

Keep these guidelines in mind when brainstorming. They can be repeated if the session bogs down or participants become judgmental.

Third, remember that the pace of thought should be quick, but not too rapid.

Fourth, make sure that your group meets in a comfortable, secure setting.

It's especially important to emphasize the nonjudgmental and noncompetitive aspects of brainstorming. People who know they won't be attacked or ridiculed will be more open and creative. An open and free environment is absolutely essential. Fear of being wrong or encountering hostility decreases spontaneous creativity.

Participant selection

Who you choose to include in a brainstorming session depends on the type of problem you have. If you have a problem in your family, or at work, or in a community or political organization, all those affected or involved in the problem should be asked to participate or be represented. Research and experience show there are several factors to consider before setting up a group.

• The intelligence level of each member.

• The backgrounds and experience of each member.

• The ideal number of people to have involved.

• The ratio of males to females in the group.

• The place and time for the session.

Intelligence. The group should be bright and well-informed. Too much contrast in intellectual skills, except among family members of different ages and abilities, may inhibit equal, comfortable exchange. When your problem is work related, try to include participants from the same employment levels. If it is a personal or family problem, differences in age, interests, and abilities are usually buffered by the presumed unity in most other matters. That presumption won't always hold, but it's more likely than not to exist.

Backgrounds and experience. Try not to mix people with vastly contrasting traits, if possible. For example, mixing shy people with outgoing people, or doers with thinkers may cause conflict rather than stimulation. When there are too many differences among participants, participants might focus on those differences rather than the problem. Bringing together people with *greatly* similar temperaments and experiences, however, may limit the group's vision and should be avoided as well.

Number of participants. In my experience, groups that include from five to seven people are very effective. When you're handling   personal, everyday problems, large groups aren't useful. A leader or coordinator should be appointed no matter how small your group is, to keep the session going. Successful brainstorming has been reported in large groups (50 to 100), and in small groups (two to three). The size of your group will depend on the number of people genuinely involved in the search for a solution to your problem.

Gender balance. Including an equal number of men and women in a session is ideal, and usually stimulates the flow of ideas. If an equal number of either sex isn't directly concerned with the problem, however, there is no need to create an artificial balance.

Place and time. If at all possible, get away from the location of the problem. The location of a brainstorming session should be different from the usual place of work or home life: a nearby resort, motel, quiet picnic area, or a special room within your home or organization. A different location helps create a free-wheeling exchange of ideas. However, there should be some real connection with the problem so the participants can work on it before and after these sessions.

LEADING A BRAINSTORMING SESSION

Try to circulate your problem statement prior to the session and write it on a blackboard or flip chart right before your session begins. You may include a few examples of the kinds of ideas that might be useful. However, be careful when introducing "start up" ideas that you don't establish a mind set. Be prepared to offer more sample ideas in case participants get bogged down. These prepared ideas should stimulate subconscious thinking. It's surprising how many solutions pop up if you don't work at them too hard!

Location

Brainstorming doesn't require total isolation to be successful. It can occur spontaneously at the breakfast table, in car pools, on airplanes, or during breaks in the day. Mini-sessions can be quite useful. Brainstorming shouldn't be a marathon to drain people of ideas. During an eight-hour work day, no more than two hours should be devoted to brainstorming. The first session should be broken into twenty-minute intervals. People are less creative when tired or stressed. Brainstorming should be intense, but not exhausting.

Preparation

Brainstorming should never be an unexpected surprise. The better prepared the coordinator and participants, the more successful they're likely to be. Spontaneity comes from deferred judgment, not from lack of preparation.

To get started or to leap over any lulls, the coordinator can try asking questions about ideas he or she has supplied or one the group has generated. Questions can be about whether the idea can be:

• Put to other uses,

• Adapted, modified, magnified, or lessened,

• Substituted, rearranged, reversed, or combined.

Authority figures

Research and experience show that when an authority figure attends a session, his or her presence usually puts a damper on participation. It's difficult to be freewheeling and noncritical if a boss or some other authority figure is on hand. It might work if the authority figure observes rather than participates, but even that's touchy. Participants must be relaxed.

Group rotation

It the problem is work or organizationally related, avoid using the same group for different problems, and having the same group work at one problem too long. There's a tendency for groups to become rigid in their approaches to brainstorming and problem solving fairly quickly. Repeated use of the same group can result in participants resorting to conventional thinking.

Seating arrangement

The seating arrangement, room layout, and decor should add to the "serious informality" of the occasion. Name tags or cards should be provided to participants if they don't already know each other. The group's leader or coordinator should be visible and reachable. There's no need to maintain any formality in seating. Allowing members to rearrange their seating literally offers them a new perspective, especially after a break. Whatever seating arrangement is decided on, each member of the brainstorming group should be able to maintain eye contact with other individuals in the session.

Response sharing

Participants should raise their hands for recognition. If several participants have their hands raised, the coordinator should move quickly from one to another in order to maintain a fast tempo. The coordinator should also discourage anyone from reading lists of ideas they prepared prior to the session because that dampens the freewheeling atmosphere.

The coordinator should allow only one idea at a time from each person, and should encourage ideas that are sparked by a previous idea. This chain reaction can be stimulated by asking participants to snap their fingers when raising their hands. If several hands are up, the coordinator should always call first on those who are snapping their fingers to encourage others to do the same.

Record ideas

It is useful to have someone keep track of the ideas. Ideas can be jotted down, or better yet, recorded on tape. If a coordinator writes a few of the ideas on a blackboard or flip chart as the session goes on, this will stimulate more ideas, encouraging new combinations or additional ideas.

If possible, each idea should be numbered. This allows participants to see the actual number produced, as well as stimulating them to come up with more ideas. Ideas shouldn't be identified with any particular person, however. The same idea may have occurred to others, or the idea may have directly resulted from a previous suggestion.

The coordinator or leader

To make sure the atmosphere of the session is freewheeling, but not trivial or foolish, the coordinator's attitude is critical. A knowledgeable coordinator is essential. In family matters, brainstorming can be done on the more informal basis of putting heads together.

Expectations

The coordinator should be careful not to expect miracles from brainstorming or to inflate its value to the group. Brainstorming, as already noted, is an aid to problem solving, not a substitute. If brainstorming is presented as a cure-all, then everyone is going to be disappointed.

Warm-up sessions

Consider starting your sessions with a brief warm-up, especially if you're working with a group that isn't familiar with brainstorming. Using jokes is an easy way to learn brainstorming, while preparing to "storm" more serious problems. A couple of the more successful problems I've posed for warm-up purposes have been:

- How many other uses can you brainstorm for a paper clip?

- If you woke up tomorrow and were twice the size you are today, what difficulties would you encounter?

In three sessions in which the second question was used, I obtained forty-seven, thirty-four, and thirty-six ideas, all within two minutes! You might also try bringing cartoons and asking the group to brainstorm captions for them within two minutes.

AVOIDING PITFALLS

There are some pitfalls to be avoided in introducing the technique of brainstorming. Again, avoid overselling the technique as a substitute for problem solving or decision making. It takes time and experience to learn to lead a brainstorming session effectively. And, it takes a certain amount of indoctrination and practice before people can participate to the full extent of their capabilities as members of a group.

A good way to initiate participants to the method is to suggest trying it as an experiment. As long as you keep your brainstorming on an experimental basis, and everybody understands and is sympathetic with this objective, you'll have the time and freedom to make mistakes, analyze them, correct them, and gain the experience you and your brainstormers will need.

Never attempt to use brainstorming as a substitute for individual thinking. Brainstorming shouldn't be used on a problem simply because an individual is too lazy to work out solutions. It may be used to supplement the work of the individual by adding to what he or she has already produced. But it is *not* a substitute for individual thinking. Avoid this pitfall at all costs!

A prime pitfall is the failure to present the problem correctly. A problem statement that's stated too broadly will cause the group to flounder and go off in too many directions. On the other hand, a problem that is too narrowly stated doesn't take advantage of brainstorming's ability to uncover many different approaches.

Two more potential problems are in the area of follow-up. Failure to take action on the group's ideas and failure to report back to the group about any successes achieved as a result of their work can lead to frustration and apathy about the brainstorming process and make future participation and cooperation difficult to obtain.

Brainstorming sessions often run smoothly. However, to fully prepare you for taking a position as a coordinator or leader of a session refer to the list below, which includes several of the difficulties we've discussed throughout this chapter, as well as additional potential problems.

- Lack of adequate preparation.

- Lack of enthusiasm and support from participants.

- Putting too much faith in brainstorming before there are any results.

- Failure to clarify the problem, or to focus on the real problem.

- Failure to warn participants that many of the first ideas offered may not be creative, and not to become discouraged.

- Failure to keep participants focused on the real problem.

- Failure to seek more details when ideas are too general.

- Failure to ask provocative, idea-spurring questions when a session slows down.

•   Failure to distinguish use of the technique from the use of individual or logical thinking.

•   Failure to distinguish between an open atmosphere and one that has strayed from the problem or has gotten out of hand.

•   Failure to evaluate and handle ideas effectively.

•   Failure to put ideas into action.

   If these potential obstacles are avoided, the value of brainstorming can be tremendous. Using a good leader or coordinator can make a great difference. After the session is over, try to get away from your problem for at least a day. Then, contact everyone again to see if they have any additional ideas. Because participants will also have "slept" on the problem, you might get some of your best ideas at this time. If additional ideas are detailed, you might want to write them down.
   After you've contacted everyone, you may want to make a list of all the ideas, breaking them down into several categories. I suggest using between five and ten categories. Some categories I have found useful are money, time, and space requirements. You can rewrite or edit these ideas as long as the original intent is not lost. In the next chapter you'll learn how to judge and select among the number of potential solutions.

10

DETERMINING THE PROS AND CONS OF YOUR SOLUTIONS

*"There is always an easy solution
to every human problem—
neat, plausible, and wrong."*

H. L. Mencken

This chapter focuses on evaluating the potential solutions you've gathered throughout the problem-solving process, and especially during your brainstorming session. The critical attitude you temporarily put aside during that session will now be useful as you assess the possible consequences of implementing those solutions. However, before trying to determine the value of your numerous solutions, review just what brainstorming can and can't do. Remember that material produced by brainstorming represents only *opportunities* that you can accept or reject.

If your problem is not complex, one of your ideas may simply solve it, and you won't have to delve any further into the evaluation process. For example, when a fuel pump on a car is defective, you replace it and you're on your way. Most problems are not so simple, however. The evaluation of potential solutions begins with asking a few questions.

- How can we judge ideas?

- How can we be sure that we'll consider the best solutions and won't overlook potentially useful possibilities?

- How can we know we won't waste time and effort on impossibilities?

We can address these questions only by turning to our objectives.

REMEMBERING YOUR OBJECTIVES

As mentioned, you suspended your judgment temporarily to generate ideas during the brainstorming process. For this reason, when you're evaluating all your options, it may be tempting to seize an idea you happen to prefer just because it *seems* like the best of all possible solutions.

This would be a risky course of action. Instead, let's shift from hot ideation to cooler judgment. If you've generated a large volume of potential solutions, evaluate them in two steps. First, evaluate them casually, dividing them into categories such as "more likely" or "less likely."

Second, focus your evaluation by measuring all of your ideas in these categories against a common yardstick. In other words, refer to your objectives. Most solutions can be evaluated by asking these typical questions as you keep your objectives in mind.

- Is the idea simple?

- Does the idea seem obvious?

- Is the idea *too* clear, *too* ingenious, or *too* complicated?

- Is the idea compatible with human nature?

- Will those who are involved in the problem accept the idea?

- Can you write out a clear, concise, two to three sentence statement about the idea?

- Does your idea seem innovative and novel?

- Does anyone react to the idea by asking, "Why didn't I think of that?"

- Is it timely, or would it have worked better six months ago?

The U.S. Navy has a list of key criteria to ask when evaluating solutions:

- Will the idea increase productivity? Improve quality?

- Will the idea mean more efficient utilization of human resource power?

- Will the idea improve methods of operation, maintenance, or construction?

- Will the idea mean an improvement over present methods?

- Will implementation of the idea improve safety?

- Does the idea prevent waste, or conserve material?

- Does the idea eliminate unnecessary work?

- Does the idea reduce cost?

- Will the idea improve working conditions?

Often the most difficult type of problems to evaluate are personal problems. The four-way test suggested by the International Rotary Club may help you in personal situations.

- Is the idea truthful?

- Is the idea fair to all concerned?

- Will the idea build goodwill and better friendship?

- Will the idea be beneficial to all concerned?

As you ask these questions, disregard the sources of your potential solutions and work to reduce the ideas to a manageable number. The previous work you did during the brainstorming session to combine and edit your solutions has already somewhat reduced their number. You may have also eliminated ideas of little obvious value in the time following your brainstorming session.

CONTINUING THE PROCESS OF ELIMINATION

Your next step is to sort potential solutions into more categories. You may decide to do this according to similarity of ideas; by the resources needed to achieve them; or by the length of time or financial resources needed to implement them. The type of problem usually suggests the categories. Time and money categories are almost invariably included among them. A more comprehensive list of categories follows.

- People requirements
- Money requirements
- Program requirements
- Facility requirements
- Evaluation requirements
- Streamlining requirements
- Training requirements
- Research requirements

- Health and wellness considerations
- Communication requirements
- Public relations considerations

If any of the potential solutions aren't clearly stated, you can revise them yourself, or get help from the person who suggested the idea. While evaluating and selecting possible solutions, you may want to restate and combine related ideas. This is all part of critical thinking.

When the list of edited and reduced ideas is completed, you and others should review it again. You will continue to narrow and reduce possible solutions through the process of elimination. Those who help you at this stage probably shouldn't be members of your brainstorming team. If they are, however, their attitudes should be more critical than they were during brainstorming. Unfortunately, finding others to participate in eliminating ideas isn't always possible or practical for personal or family problems.

Problem Solving Tip # 19

Remember that choosing among alternatives often demands courage and moral judgment as well as intelligence— one alternative you should always consider is that you could be wrong.
Joseph J. Bannon

Richard Lyles, in *Practical Management Problem Solving* further illustrates,

"Don't do anything solely because it worked once before. Choose actions that are clearly justified based on the demands of the current problem situation" (p. 131).

Compare your possible solutions with the must and want, and factual and value objectives you decided on earlier. Never lose sight of your objectives. In fact, keep them on hand and within sight throughout the problem-solving process. Try to maintain three topic worksheets throughout the problem-solving process.

1.   **Your problem statement**
2.   **Your objectives**
3.   **The list of solutions you're considering.**

Because objectives are yardsticks for screening and evaluating potential solutions, they should be modified only with *very* good reason, or your efforts at problem solving could self-destruct. Never change your objectives to match a solution that merely *appeals* to you. If your objectives are based on hard facts and on your core values, they should remain fairly constant.

If you lightly and carelessly reorder your objectives, you may not be prepared for the consequences. You must not only be concerned with what you will be taking on, but also with what you will be giving up or sacrificing.

CONSIDERING CONSEQUENCES

You're basically interested in one solution or a mix of related solutions to your problem. You're seeking the *best* solution, or the one that most appropriately solves your problem, which isn't always your preferred solution. Try not to favor solutions that merely appeal to you or sound exciting, regardless of their relationship to your objectives.

At this point, brainstorming can be useful again to discover the pros and cons of each remaining potential solution. Brainstorm about the risks involved in selecting a particular solution and the risks involved in *not* selecting it. It may be beneficial to conduct a brainstorming session on what is *wrong* with potential solutions and another session on what is *right* with them.

Because you're closer to the problem and have better hunches about the value of the ideas you are considering, brainstorming at this stage is likely to be quick and smooth. At this point, categorize the pros and cons and rights and wrongs of your potential solutions. Then edit them in the same way the original ideas were edited.

As you continue to select and evaluate solutions, consider the possible consequences of each. Think about and record the risks of using or not using each one. I like to use a notebook or account book at this stage to describe probable consequences of implementing or not implementing a solution. It's helpful to have notes to refresh your memory when you come back to the problem, and notes can also help you clarify your ideas when you share them with others.

In considering consequences, evaluate the current problem situation as well as the future situation. Again, take into account the perspectives, perceptions, and expectations of everyone involved. Also, try to anticipate the potential impact of each potential solution on the environments in which you operate, including your office, home, religious facility, and community center.

For example, let's assume you've selected as an option sending your daughter to a small college to further her education. Obviously, there are consequences in selecting this option. You need to carefully examine these before implementing any action. Figure 10.1 clarifies this point.

Now think again of the individual in Chapter Six who was considering a move to Seattle, Washington. We would all agree that a major move needs to be thought through carefully. All of the positives and negatives need to be scrutinized. Figure 10.2 examines the consequences of selecting this option.

Figure 10.1
Pro and Con Option Evaluation

<u>Option</u>   <u>Consequences</u>

Send daughter to   1. Pros
small college
                                • Less chance of campus
                                  crime
                                • Better security
                                • Smaller student-instructor
                                  ratios
                                • More personal attention

                            2. Cons

                                • Lack of financial resources
                                • Fewer distinguished faculty
                                • Lack of computer technology

Selecting a solution demands candid assessments of the consequences of your decision. Not doing anything about your problem is a real option. As discussed in Chapter Two, many people take this option frequently. Unfortunately, too often they fail to examine the consequences of this decision.

Evaluating potential solutions is basically a screening process. In a way, it's like panning gold. There may be a lot of grit and dirt for every nugget. The solution that appears to be the best solution should be examined carefully to make sure it's appropriate and adequate.

Figure 10.2
Pro and Con Option Evaluation

<u>Option</u>   <u>Consequences</u>

Move to Seattle, Washington 1. Pros

- Increased career potential
- Increased income
- Enhanced job variety
- New job skills
- Improved living environment
- Life style differences

2. Cons

- Create family disruption
- Difficulty of spouse employment
- Increase in cost of living
- Undesirable weather and climate
- Disrupt established relationships
- Life style differences

It takes time and careful thought to anticipate how a particular action may impact the rest of our world, or environment. However, we must try to anticipate consequences and, to some extent, control them. As we've seen many times in regard to oil spills, consequences are especially critical when they affect the natural environment.

NARROWING YOUR FOCUS

As you zero in on ideas that may be suitable solutions to your problem, you can categorize them in several ways. It's often useful to categorize them according to whether they are long- or short-term solutions. Are you looking for a solution with a lasting impact, or do you require a solution that might give you more immediate benefits?

Problem Solving Tip #20

If the problem you are solving is of serious concern, the more careful you should be with the decision. "Sleep on it" is often wise advice to follow before committing yourself to a serious decision. This is especially true when emotions are involved.

Joseph J. Bannon

As Michael Sanderson, author of *Successful Problem Management*, stated,

"Before we put a solution into effect, we must be sure it is the best one. Preferably we will have thought of more than one solution to the problem, each with its own peculiar advantages. Badly thought-out solutions cause at least as much harm as having done nothing" (p. 31).

If your main concern is money, or people, or time, then concentrate on the appropriate category. Ask yourself if you seek an inexpensive solution, or a quick one? Ask yourself how you can get the money to implement your solution. Can you get the money, but not the people to help?

Remember that if you feel a solution is necessary and that you're most suited to providing it, you'll be more willing to struggle to get the necessary resources. During the process of struggle, however, don't lose sight of the solution's consequences. Rushing to get what you want is admirable under some circumstances and foolhardy under others. Although I don't advise you to be overly prudent, acting without forethought can be disastrous.

RESEARCHING PREVIOUS SOLUTIONS

Because many of your potential solutions may have been tried before in similar circumstances, try to find out how they worked for others. Although, as stated previously, you shouldn't discard potential solutions because they've failed in other situations or when implemented by other people, it may be valuable to study the circumstances surrounding past failures and successes.

You can gather information on successes and failures from friends, family members, coworkers, club members, colleagues, and acquaintances, or from case studies, library materials and various governmental and municipal agencies. If you enjoy detective work and research, this stage of problem solving should be very interesting for you.

The momentum is in your favor now, because you've become an expert on your problem situation. You can speak with conviction and share information confidently. It's a good feeling to close in on a solution. As well as helping us to solve everyday problems, methodical problem solving can reveal strengths we may not have realized in ourselves. It can also make us aware of thought patterns and methods we can use to help us get things done.

As you research previous solutions to your problem, don't overlook those that weren't successful. They may offer valuable information, especially about unhappy consequences. However, don't rely exclusively on the experiences of others. It's important to come to your own conclusions, based on the information and experience you have.

Continue to reduce the number of solutions you're considering. Considering four or five solutions is the norm, as most of us don't have the resources to evaluate too many more. There are times when one solution is as good as another. In these cases a search for a better one is a waste of effort. Sometimes taking action on an acceptable solution is more desirable than delaying to secure a better solution. Perfectionists often make poor decision makers.

Considering options and making choices among them is a major part of problem solving. Selecting solutions is an exciting, demanding, and challenging process. Try to remember the following two caveats.

1.   *Choosing among alternatives sometimes demands courage and moral judgment as well as intelligence.*

2.   *After all your evaluation, you may still choose the wrong solution.*

Most of the hard work is behind us now, and we're ready to tackle the final steps of problem solving. As you review the previous chapters, you may still consider problem solving too time consuming. Just try to remember that you'll be able to implement its steps faster each time you use this method. In Chapter Eleven, we'll examine the qualities and traits of decision makers and what goes into making decisions.

11

CHOOSING THE BEST SOLUTION

*"There are two types of solutions
to every problem; you can do
something about the problem,
or you can do nothing about it.
Not taking any action to solve the
problem is a course of action;
you have postponed or ignored the problem."*

Joseph J. Bannon

By now, you've defined your problem, clarified your objectives, considered potential problem-solving obstacles, and evaluated and reduced the total number of possible solutions. Your next task will be to decide which solution is best for your problem. This means you must take on the role of being a decision maker as well as a problem solver.

BECOMING A DECISION MAKER

Decision making involves more risk and responsibility than any other aspect of problem solving. Few problems have a single solution. In fact, there are usually several promising courses of action, and it becomes necessary to make a choice from among them. Decision making often requires that we try to predict results of events that haven't occurred yet.

Responsibility

A decision maker must accept full responsibility for a chosen solution. Even if a decision is made by a group, any risk involved in the outcome is almost always managed by one or two people. The work of problem analysis and evaluation can be delegated, but the responsibility of decision making is yours alone. When it's time to decide on a course of action, the buck stops with you.

In many families and organizations, the same person isn't responsible for problem analysis and evaluation. This is especially true of large organizations and personal and social groups where the leader or coordinator is too busy to undertake this work. In a work situation, you may be responsible for defining a problem and offering one or more solutions to a decision maker. Or, you may be in the position of having others do the preliminary work for you.

Cooperation

It's useful to have more than one person handle problem analysis. If we try to do everything ourselves, or delegate too much to a single person, we'll see how unproductive overloading can be. When problems occurred in simpler, less chaotic times, a single person handling a problem from start to finish may have been successful. However, today most actions involve or affect others, or perhaps we've simply become more aware of the effects of private and public decisions.

Whoever the decision maker is, under ideal conditions, he or she will try to solve the problem by selecting from well-researched and well-documented solutions. The image of a decision maker is often that of an executive who delegates problem analysis, then quickly examines the information received to reach a decision, which is quickly put into effect and without fail is a success! In reality, decision making and the people involved in the process are somewhat less glorified. Today, we can all benefit from the expertise and insights of others. It may seem to be simpler and quicker to work alone, but our results may not be as effective as those we could obtain by working cooperatively.

AVOIDING GROUPTHINK AND OTHER PROBLEMS

Irving Janis, in his book *Groupthink*, warns that when groups get together to make a decision, they should be careful of being caught in the "Groupthink Syndrome." According to this concept, members of any small cohesive group tend to maintain esprit de corps by unconsciously developing a number of shared illusions and related norms that interfere with critical thinking.

An important symptom of groupthink is accepting the illusion of being invulnerable to dangers that might arise from risky action in which the group is strongly tempted to engage. Essentially, the notion is that if the leader and everyone else in our group decides it's OK, our solution to the problem will succeed.

Janis contends that the Watergate cover-up was a classic case of groupthink. He believes evidence indicates that prior to and during the planning of the Watergate cover-up Nixon, Haldeman and Ehrlichman felt bound by mutual ties and commitments to common goals, which resulted in a keen sense of loyalty and an absolute adherence to a shared set of norms.

Janis describes other situations characteristic of the groupthink syndrome, including the Bay of Pigs invasion, the bombing of Pearl Harbor, and the conflicts in Vietnam and Korea. Janis states that there are eight symptoms that may warn us that we're falling in the trap of groupthink.

1. An illusion of invulnerability, shared by most or all the members, which creates excessive optimism and encourages taking extreme risks.

2.   An unquestioned belief in the group's inherent morality, inclining the members to ignore the ethical or moral consequences of their decisions.

3.   Collective efforts to rationalize in order to discount warnings or other information that might lead the members to reconsider their assumptions before they recommit themselves to their past policy decisions.

4.   Stereotyped views of enemy leaders as too evil to warrant genuine attempts to negotiate, or as too weak and stupid to counter whatever risky attempts are made to defeat their purposes.

5.   Self-censorship of deviations from the apparent group consensus, reflecting each member's inclination to minimize to himself the importance of his doubts and counterarguments.

6.   A shared illusion of unanimity concerning judgments conforming to the majority view (partly resulting from self-censorship of deviations, augmented by the false assumption that silence means consent).

7.   Direct pressure on any member who expresses strong arguments against any of the group's stereotypes, illusions, or commitments, making clear that this type of dissent is contrary to what is expected of all loyal members.

8.   The emergence of self-appointed mind guards — members who protect the group from adverse information that might shatter their shared complacency about the effectiveness and morality of their decisions.

A review of these eight symptoms may remind you of situations that you've encountered. The groupthink syndrome is evidenced in city hall council chambers, state legislatures, Congress, clubs and organizations to which we belong, places we work, as well as in family and home situations.

A number of authors who study the decision-making process have suggested numerous causes of careless decision making. Below is a list of the most common reasons:

- Lack of clear objectives
- Inattention to earlier stages of problem solving
- Ignorance of better methods
- Laziness
- Complacency
- Prejudice
- Recency of similar problems
- Over-reliance on past experience
- Copying other people's decisions
- Impulsive reactions to events
- Irresponsible indulgence of whims and fancies
- Pursuit of private or irrelevant objectives
- Uncritical pursuit of the obvious
- Taking the easy way out

You've probably noticed that several of the items on this list
are similar to the blocks to creativity. You can learn to avoid them
by re-examining bad decisions and identifying the items on the
list that may have had an effect on your decision-making process.

CHOICES TODAY AND IN THE FUTURE

The problem-solving method used in this book reflects the
kind of problems you may experience now and those you may
encounter in the future. The type of decision maker needed then
and now will be one who can respond to rapid change. The
decision maker of the future will be increasingly involved with
and dependent upon others. Because interaction is a major factor
in creative thinking, this should enhance our problem-solving
skills and abilities.

Nothing is more valuable in making decisions than a broad
knowledge base. Effective decision makers must understand
large systems and environments, other societies and cultures,
and national and international concerns. Decision makers now

and in the future will also need to understand computers and related technologies. Because technology is changing rapidly, this will require a robust effort.

We should be open to changes in the world around us — those close to us and those distant, those intimate and those more impersonal. We'll need to be adaptive, flexible, and creative to keep pace with the future. Our understanding of change should include a willingness to modify our own behavior, as well as the behavior of other group members. It's not enough to sympathize with the need for change; we must be ready to change.

Making decisions that ignore important psychological, political, social, or other forces can mean failure in problem solving. The blocks to problem solving we discussed, including personal prejudices, will come up again. If you have difficulty responding to various changes in your life because of personal or cultural blocks, your skill in decision making will be impaired.

No matter how logical we think we are, emotions will always have weight in our decisions. It will be useful for us to remember that effective decision makers are influenced more by positive than negative emotions and that they attempt to resolve negative attitudes before reaching a decision.

ACHIEVING A MIND-HEART BALANCE

Decision making is the most dramatic stage of problem solving, and is complete only when a course of action has been chosen, and a commitment has been made to carry it out. Some regard decision making as the essence of all problem solving. Whether or not this perspective is absolutely true in all cases, it's wise to take the care in making decisions that it implies.

Problem Solving Tip #21

Make a decision only when you adequately understand the pertinent facts and the ramifications of your solution.
Joseph J. Bannon

In the next few pages, we'll discuss how to take all of these factors into consideration before committing to a decision about your best solution.

Situation variables

One of the worst decision-making mistakes is to announce a decision impulsively before all the information has been collected. Victor Vroom, professor of psychology at Yale University, suggests we first ask ourselves a series of questions about what he calls "situation variables."

1. *Rational Quality Requirement*
    Does it make a difference which course of action is adopted?

2. *Adequacy of Information*
    Does the problem solver have the adequate information to make a quality analysis?

3. *Structure of Situation*
    Does the problem solver know exactly what information is missing and how to get the information?

4. *Commitment Requirement*
    Is commitment to the solution by others critical to effective implementation?

5. *Commitment without Participation*
    Will they commit to a decision made by the problem solver without their active participation?

6. *Goal Congruence*
    Is there goal congruence between all those affected by the decision?

7. *Conflict about Alternatives*
    Is there likely to be conflict about alternative solutions among those concerned?

8. *Subordinate Competency*
    Do the people involved have the skill and know-how to implement the idea suggested?

Analysis of self and others

The best way to achieve a mind-heart balance in decision making is to know yourself and others involved in the problem. Considering personal motives and preconceptions is very beneficial. This sort of personal and political knowledge of yourself and others can be helpful throughout the problem-solving process, including later when you put your selected solution into effect.

The more time you give to understanding possible personal barriers to decision making, the better prepared you'll be for difficulties. You don't have to do an in-depth psychological analysis of yourself and others, however. A candid appraisal of your own shortcomings and those of others involved in the problem will suffice. You should also be aware of potentially disruptive emotional situations, so they don't distort or interfere with your decision making.

You know to some extent what your prejudices are, and how you can realistically deal with them. You must try to understand what personal drives, needs, and compulsions motivate everyone else involved in the problem situation. This is critical when making decisions crucial to your own well-being and that of others. Try not to let emotions blind you to the strength or weakness of any solution.

In examining the emotions and drives of others, you should use the same approach as you did when analyzing yourself. Don't pressure others with lectures about the negative influence of emotions. Instead, try to find out what emotions influence them, and work with them individually and tactfully.

Try to lead by example. How you handle your own emotions will impress others — either negatively or positively. Your aim is to be an effective, balanced decision maker. As an all-around, well-adjusted person, you may be popular with others and ignore their failings. However, you'll lack the sharp edge of insight and criticism needed to make good decisions.

Spontaneous decisions

Situations do arise in which there is no opportunity to use the problem-solving method. We may have to make a sudden decision while playing bridge, or during a physical sport, or decision while playing bridge, or during a physical sport, or when someone puts a question to us in conversation. In these circumstances, we rely largely on intuition and habit. Yet, there's usually time to identify the type of decision with which we are faced. To do this, reduce the problem to its most elementary state by asking this question: Is it more important to avoid failure or to go all out for success?

The answer to this question will help you make your decision. Figure 11.1, Anatomy of a Decision, provides a visual description of this condensed, time-driven process.

Figure 11.1
Anatomy of a Decision

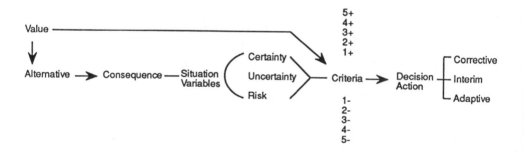

Risks

An effective decision maker is able to take risks and to encourage others to do so as well. As I've emphasized throughout this book, when you make a decision, you must consider the viewpoints of all involved in the problem situation. This is a political skill, which, at times, may detract from your willingness to take risks.

You may be tempted to concentrate more on reducing conflict and strengthening the group or family spirit than on the need to take a chance. The role of the decision maker is to these activities make for better decisions. A harmonious group isn't necessarily an effective group.

UNDERSTANDING YOUR OPTIONS

Your solution may not help you reach all your objectives immediately. Your objectives are actually mile posts against which you can measure your progress to your ultimate goals. This is why objectives shouldn't be vague or too flexible.

It may be necessary to compromise on *how many* of your objectives you achieve with your first solution, or even on *how close* you come to achieving them, but you should be very reluctant to compromise on the content of your objectives. After all, your original objectives, if well-considered, reflect your core values and most favored results.

When you select a solution to help you reach your objectives, you should know what options are still available. There are three kinds of options: *corrective, adaptive,* and *interim* actions. A corrective action is one that fully solves your problem. The success of most solutions is not as frequent as many t.v. programs and commercials would lead us to believe.

An adaptive action usually means deciding to live with a problem by changing the environment in which the problem exists. Some problems have no solution, or at least, no immediate solution. However, coming to the conclusion that your problem has no solution is risky. Sometimes we want to believe there is nothing we can do just to avoid doing something wrong. Before coming to such a decision, consider what consequences may follow your *inaction*.

Problem Solving Tip #22

When it comes time to make a decision, you shouldn't get too old over them. Sure they won't all be perfect. In fact, some of them will be duds. Learn from them, but don't stop trying.

Lee Iacocca

William Knaus, author of *Do It Now*, elaborated on a similar concept:

> "When making a decision to put something off, first pause to check the long-term effects of that decision. Could the decision, for example, end in an unnecessary crisis? This stop-check technique, used consistently, helps to make clear the impact that putting things off may have" (p.103).

Interim actions are temporary actions that affect problem situations quickly. Interim actions are usually coupled with plans for a corrective action later. An example of an interim action is temporarily plugging a hole in the roof while planning to repair it properly when time and resources become available.

When a problem is serious, interim actions are sometimes taken before we even begin problem solving. Interim solutions may be quite costly, but when we're faced with a dangerous or rapidly deteriorating situation, we may have little choice about relying on them. Although interim actions reduce a problem's symptoms, they're only stopgap solutions.

Decisions can also be a combination of actions. You may take interim action immediately and corrective action later. It may be necessary to employ several options to have time to find an appropriate solution to a problem.

WEIGHING THE CONSEQUENCES

Life comes without guarantees. It's impossible to solve problems without taking risks. We can only choose the course of action that seems to offer the highest probability of success with the least amount of risk. We can either accept or reject the belief that it's wise to play the odds, to put our trust in the solutions that produce at least satisfactory results most frequently. Perhaps that's why great football coaches rarely "go for it" with fourth and one.

Decisions are made on the basis of known and unknown odds.   General Schwartzkopf made many such decisions during the war with Iraq that required him to consider questionable information about weather conditions, movement of enemy troops, and the efficiency and capability of Iraq's soldiers. The risks he took meant life or death for many Allied troops. His decisions had magnitude.

In our personal lives, we also take risks that affect our own and others' lives. Should we continue our present relationship? What action should we take with a son or daughter who is taking drugs or drinking alcohol? Should we move to another job? Should we remarry? Each decision we make will have its risks.

When we make any decision, one of three elements will always exist: certainty, uncertainty, and risk. When the flashlight doesn't work, it may require just replacing the batteries, and then we can predict that we'll have light. However, if we mishandle reprimanding our child, we're uncertain about how he or she may react. If we don't handle this situation with at least some care, our long-term relationship with that child could be affected.

The greatest challenge problem solvers face is trying to determine the degree of risk and then acting accordingly. In situations that are fairly certain, definite plans can be made. In situations where a high degree of uncertainty exists, flexible plans that can be adjusted to accommodate changing conditions are more appropriate.

Earlier when you began to evaluate your potential solutions, you noted all the possible consequences — pro and con — of each idea. You now have to weigh these consequences more precisely. To evaluate your solutions, determine which of them best meets the following challenges.

1. Does this solution account for human and financial resources required?

2. Of all the options I'm considering, does this solution have the least disadvantages?

3. Of all the options I'm considering, does this solution have the greatest advantages for my problem situation?

Often, solutions to problems cost money. If you haven't estimated the resource and human cost for each possible solution, this is the time to do it. If money isn't the object, you might still indicate the cost without considering it a limitation.

To evaluate the consequences of each solution one more time, ask three questions.

1.   Can I afford this solution?

2.   How many advantages and disadvantages does this solution offer?

3.   How many people are needed to make this solution work?

Rate each solution with a plus or minus in regard to your answers to these questions. The plus or minus, or resource and people figure given to each solution doesn't have to be permanent. You can revise these ratings as you think more about the problem. For example, the short-range cost of a particular solution might be within your means. However, if the solution requires annual payments and sacrifices, that may be an entirely different matter.

Estimate the short- and long-term impact of each solution you're seriously considering. These estimates will be valuable when you're ready to make your ultimate decision. As you reject solutions that don't meet your requirements, examine them to make sure they aren't real options. Finally, be careful that the solution you pick doesn't create another or larger problem.

You're ready to make your final choice! Delay beyond this point is no longer fruitful. However, your job isn't over yet. You must prepare for any resistance your decision might bring from others. You must also be prepared to "sell" your selection to others and come up with a way of putting it into action. These concerns are the subject of the next chapter.

12

DEVELOPING SUCCESSFUL IMPLEMENTATION STRATEGIES

"Implementation of an average idea is far superior to thinking of an outstanding idea and not doing anything about it."

Joseph J. Bannon

Ideas are valuable only when we put them to use. It's easy to spend too much time generating solutions and not enough time implementing them. Too many people are quick to come up with solutions and slow to put them into action. Perhaps they consider implementation to be an automatic part of problem solving that takes care of itself.

No matter how good your idea is, there will always be a few people who will object to it and resist it. Many great ideas have been received with opposition. Columbus couldn't have discovered America if he hadn't been able to convince his crew the earth was round. Edison, Pasteur, the Wright Brothers, and other great innovators were also thought of as eccentric, unconventional, and unorthodox.

SELLING YOUR SOLUTION

This is why once you've decided on a solution, you must be prepared to "sell" it. Becoming familiar and comfortable with persuasion tactics is a must. This means planning your implementation thoroughly, presenting your ideas clearly, listening to responses attentively, and persuading others to accept your idea as the best solution. You must learn to be assertive without being obnoxious, and to always remain patient with those who object to your ideas.

These skills don't come automatically, or even naturally to most of us. However, we can acquire them with time, knowledge, and a solid commitment to our solutions. You probably already have the talent and interest to master these skills, or you wouldn't have read this much of this book.

In my workshops I always ask the participants to write down the number of good ideas they've had that have failed. When they explore the reasons for failure, they invariably include lack of planning and preparation regarding effective strategies for implementation.

Before you can put your solution to work, you have to plan how to achieve successful implementation. You can combine one or several approaches to do this. These approaches usually involve several aspects for selling the idea:

- Inform others of your solution.

- Persuade them of its value and effectiveness.

- Convince them it is the best solution under the circumstances.

- Let them know how much consideration went into selecting this particular solution over others.

- Overcome their resistance to change.

- Be prepared for emotional and cultural blocks to come up again.

Idea salesmanship is exactly what's needed if you expect resistance to your solution. Research and experience show there is resistance to change and new ideas on the part of most people. Your enthusiasm for a particular solution may be based more on its likelihood of solving your problem, than on its superiority in the eyes of others.

You must be prepared for the possibility that others may not find the solution as attractive and useful as you do. If someone comes up with a better idea, or a legitimate objection to your idea, you should be prepared to reconsider your final solution. It doesn't pay to push ahead without considering the objections of others. Doing so will only mean building barriers between you and others, and your solution's effectiveness will suffer.

Selling a solution doesn't require high-pressure tactics or deception. It involves using your enthusiasm and faith in your solution to create a climate of acceptance for your idea. If your analysis of the problem and its related factors has been thorough, you should be quite confident about your solution. If you've carefully analyzed members of your group as well as other factors related to your solution and its consequences, that information will be crucial to you now.

Problem Solving Tip #23

Prepare to sell your solution and to meet resistance from those who don't share your enthusiasm for the change it may bring.

Joseph J. Bannon

As Michael Sanderson, in *Successful Problem Management* writes:

> "A solution starts from an idea which gives it shape and unity. But the idea is only the start. It is more of an abstraction, a skeleton, or framework. Now we must carefully put together all the pieces of the real world situation around our new idea" (p. 29).

UNDERSTANDING RESISTANCE

As discussed before, change is likely to be resisted, even by those who may benefit from it! Individual needs and desires for recognition can become barriers to implementing your solution. These needs can be physical, emotional, intellectual, creative, psychological, economic, social, and cultural.

Individual needs should be anticipated and met if possible. Ignoring them will only hinder your implementation efforts. You can offset resistance and respond to misconceptions by discussing both the advantages and disadvantages of your solution. Of course, you'll emphasize the advantages to encourage acceptance of your idea. Figure 12.1 details how you can establish a climate for acceptance of your solution.

Objections will depend on the status, experience, perceptions, and self-concepts of the people raising them. Sometimes those raising objections have been influenced by what they've already heard about your solution. You can respond to these prejudgments by answering them, evading them, replacing them with substitute objections, or agreeing with them. But you must respond in some way.

Most problem-solving experts agree that objections must be dealt with if a solution is to be successfully implemented. Mastering this skill will enable you to handle difficult situations. In handling objections, two principles apply. First, every objection should be viewed as an opportunity and an advantage. This is because you will usually have an opportunity to analyze the objection, counter it, and reply in such a manner as to turn the objection into an advantage.

For example, when a real estate agent hears that a potential buyer of a brick house thinks it will be too expensive to consider,

Figure 12.1
The Climate for Idea Acceptance

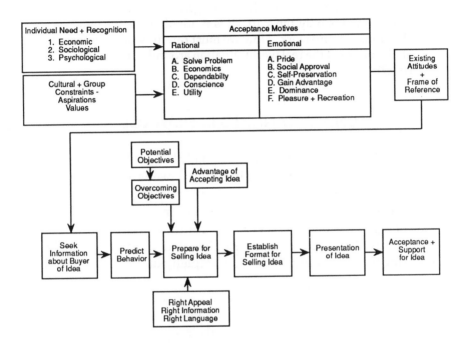

he or she can respond that a brick house is less expensive in the long run, because brick requires no painting, reduces heating and cooling costs, and has a better resale value than most other materials.

The second principle is that every objection should be seen as an opportunity to analyze the doubter's viewpoint. Recognizing others' viewpoints is essential for success. For example, when you're attempting to get a smoker to become a nonsmoker, you must try to understand why smoking is important to him or her. Some smokers fear they will gain weight if they quit their habit. Some rely on smoking to cope with stress. A teenager may be responding to peer pressure.

By understanding others' points of view, you can develop better strategies for overcoming their objections. Figure 12.2 assists in clarifying this concept.

Figure 12.2
The Perspectives of Others

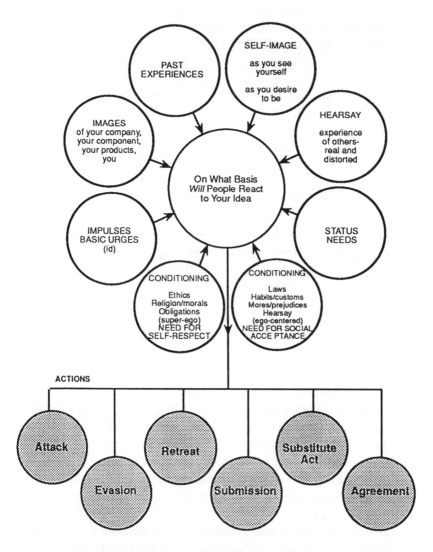

Adapted from *Salesmanship* by F.A. Russell, F.B. Beach, and R.H. Buskirk, McGraw Hill Book Company, New York, 1978, Tenth Edition.

RESPONDING TO OBJECTIONS

Several tactics can be used to respond to objections. The most effective is to anticipate them and raise them yourself! When you do this, you're fully prepared to respond. If you have answers in advance, you'll gain acceptance more easily than if you seem unprepared and surprised by doubters' questions. Use your imagination to anticipate all possible objections. You'll probably discover that you anticipated many of their objections when you considered the consequences of your solution.

There can be at least eleven kinds of objections to any new idea. I call them the "negative eleven":

1. **The idea actually costs too much.** You need to reevaluate your estimates of required human and capital investment.
2. **The idea is believed to cost too much, based on misconceptions or misinformation.** You need to share your estimates of cost and how you arrived at them.
3. **Others do not see the urgency of agreeing to a solution and putting it into effect.** You need to convey to them a sense of urgency about the problem.
4. **Others have fears about making the wrong decision.** You need to convince others that your decision is the best, based on a good deal of analysis and investigation, and that you are prepared to take full responsibility for it.
5. **Others seem dissatisfied with the idea.** If you have argued your case poorly, your argument needs to be strengthened.
6. **The idea is not practical.** This occurs when others are not convinced by your evidence, regardless its worth.
7. **Others believe the idea is not practical.** This may be due to poor presentation on your part, or not handling objections properly.
8. **Others may be strongly committed to their own solution, regardless of its merits.** This may simply be a lack of information on their part. If so, you can provide more detail.
9. **The idea is full of weaknesses you did not anticipate.** This means that it was not handled properly during the problem-solving process.

10.   **No one wants to commit themselves to future action on the problem.** Again, you need to create a sense of urgency about the problem and its need for a solution, as well as to demonstrate your willingness to put it into action.

11.   **Not everyone is convinced of the value of your solution.** You need to prepare for ways to stimulate others' excitement about the problem and to enhance their interest in your solution.

Four additional tactics, some of which have been mentioned earlier are discussed in detail below.

1.   **Agree with the objection and turn it into a selling point.** This should be done honestly, without deception.

2.   **Discover the reason for the objection.** It may be a point that you completely overlooked. Never assume that familiarity with a problem makes you infallible.

3.   **Admit the objection may be valid.** As with all tactics, this one should only be used honestly — when the objection is valid, not merely when it's convenient to smooth ruffled feathers.

4.   **Meet the objection.** Present information or arguments to disprove it.

DISCOVERING SMOKE SCREENS

Objections may be raised for valid reasons, or they may be part of a hidden agenda. A stated objection may be a smoke screen that covers a real objection. Someone may want to introduce ambiguity, uncertainty, and confusion. Because the objector or doubter isn't stating his or her real objection, you will have difficulty discerning what that objection is and how to handle it.

Reasons for establishing smoke screens vary. Unknown motives can present roadblocks to implementation that may be impossible to overcome. If the smoke screen can't be removed, successful problem solving may be impossible. Figure 12.3 may help explain how unknown motives may sabotage implementation.

Figure 12.3
A Model of the Hidden Motive Obstacle

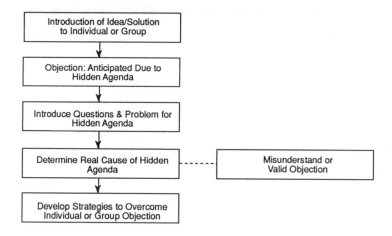

Before you present the solution to others for their response or approval, you need to set goals for what you want to occur. In the next section, we'll examine this process.

GETTING WHAT YOU WANT

To get what you want, define your **want** and **must goals** for responses from others. Do this the same way you defined your value and factual objectives. However, remember that although it's appropriate to resist compromise on objectives, you should be open to compromise on these **want** and **must goals**. You aren't compromising your desires and values; you're coming to an agreement on how your solution will be implemented. In other words, be prepared to accept alternative methods for implementing your solution, while keeping your major objectives intact.

Problem Solving Tip #24

Successful decisions are more than good
decisions. Once made, decisions must
be implemented effectively to obtain the
desired goals and solve the problem.
                    Harvey J. Brightman

If you continue to encounter resistance, you could ask
others, or a committee, to study the problem. This will demonstrate your confidence in the solution and your sincerity about
involving others in the problem-solving process. If you're clever,
you may even convince others that it was their idea to study the
matter further. If you do this, make sure something is decided on.
You're responsible for directing the course and the outcome of
your solution.

Timing

In preparing for objections, consider the best time for
presenting your ideas. Unless you're facing a critical situation,
avoid times when others are busy, tired, or short of funds or
personnel. For example, a friend of mine wants to take a leave of
absence from his job. He decided on this solution to his stress
problem, after considering the consequences of his request. He
has also waited until his workload was low. If he submitted his
request when the tempo of work was fast, it would have probably
remained at the bottom of someone's in-basket.

Timing is even more important in urgent situations. Remember that just because you're ready for change doesn't mean
everyone else is. My friend is in a one-of-a-kind position with his
company, so his absence would be resisted under the best of
circumstances. He jokingly told me his request for a six-months'
leave would probably be approved if he took it every other day.

You can see that much of the work in getting a solution accepted is done *before* it's submitted to others. In fact, it's at this stage of the problem-solving process that you'll spend the most energy on behind-the-scenes preparation. You'll have to be as alert as possible to the many contingencies that might develop.

Preparation

Your preparedness will show others that you have given much consideration to your problem. At this point, you must thoroughly understand your solution, be able to defend it, explain how objections to it can be met, and discuss how you intend to implement it. The following tips may help you sell your ideas.

- **Make the advantages of the solution obvious to others.** If my friend's employer can't see the benefits of granting a leave to a stressed worker, he will have to point out that his present value and productivity as well as his potential future contributions may be jeopardized by resistance to his request for a sabbatical.

- **Satisfy the needs of those who will benefit from the solution.** Because my friend's job is unique in his business, he has long urged the company to train others so he doesn't face a backlog whenever he is absent. His leave could benefit the company in two ways. One, he will stay longer with the company if he has some control over his physical and mental well-being. Two, the leave would provide an opportunity to try others in the job. If others did well, the company would have more options in dealing with his future absences.

- **Indicate the economic value of your idea.**

- **Build on the support and enthusiasm you may already have from those in favor of your idea.** You shouldn't become so concerned about objections from opponents to your solution that you forget to bolster existing support.

- **If the problem is at work or in a community organization, you should prepare audiovisual displays.** The technologies in videos and computer graphics, for instance, are really expanding, so you should keep informed and take advantage of them.

- **Work to make the change acceptable to as many as possible.** No idea will be accepted by everyone. Concentrate on winning over the majority of people involved in the problem situation.

- **Be convinced of your own decision before trying to sell it to others.** If you don't buy it, no one else will.

- **Back up your decision with good facts, research, and know-how.** There is no substitute for information. Others will want to know just what you based your decision on, and why they should commit their energies to implementing it.

- **Don't criticize those who object to or resist your idea.** Negative campaigning only seems to work in politics. At some point you may need the support of your detractors.

- **Don't get excited or emotional if anyone resists your suggestion.** Calm, reasoned responses will convince others of your confidence more quickly than angry rebuttals.

- **Don't debate your idea, sell it.** Don't become so involved in refuting objections that you forget to emphasize your solution's "positives."

- **Don't distort the worth or impact of your solution.** Be realistic about what it can achieve, and others will be more likely to trust your assessment of the solution's real worth.

- **Be willing to compromise on how your solution is put into action.** While my friend doesn't want his six-months' leave every other day for a year, he is willing to compromise on when it starts and how long it lasts. He didn't announce that to his supervisors, but his willingness will keep him flexible when bargaining and be less likely to add to his stress!

• **Don't be in a hurry for agreement or approval.** Give others time to mull your solution over and get used to your idea.

• **Be ready to change your mind about your solution.** Be willing to discard it, if necessary. My friend has considered that he may not need a leave if he gets someone to help him who could be trained for the job, or if he can get a temporary or permanent transfer to another position in the company.

Written reports and other aids

How you present your solution depends on for whom it is intended. If your solution is intended to solve a family or a social club problem, audiovisuals and written reports probably aren't necessary. If it's intended to solve a problem related to work or to a civic project, these aids may be very effective.

By preparing a written report, you can share your consideration of the problem with others and clarify your own thinking through the act of writing. You will have something tangible to hand to others for future reference and clarification. A written report or memo can be given out prior to any meeting, so all parties are prepared and well informed.

It's much harder to write than to talk. Since writing makes more demands on a person's abilities than does talking, many people either are unwilling to meet these demands or are frightened by them. Writing requires that you think through the whole of what you want to say before you write a word. You have to do this in order to realize what your essential point is and how to organize your material. Doing this demands sustained thought as you work out all the parts, move them around in your mind, and relate them to each other.

Talking about your ideas is much easier, because you only have to develop a remark at a time. The other person's remarks guide you in organizing your material while you're responding to the questions and objections that are raised. In writing you have to make sure you're expressing yourself clearly. The receiver of your memo may not be there to ask you questions. Because familiarity with your idea makes it easy for you to overestimate your clarity, you run the risk of leaving something out.

When writing a report, abide by the rules of grammar, punctuation, and spelling. Writing requires physical effort, which means it can be tiring. It may be difficult to hold onto your thoughts, because writing lags behind thinking to a greater degree than does talking. You generally have to be more careful about what you put in writing because it is a permanent record. Writing requires meeting higher standards than does free-flowing discussion, because the writer has time to plan and create an entire presentation.

These standards and seeming inconveniences may be just what you need to carefully and methodically analyze your presentation — even if you decide to make an oral report instead! Meeting these demands doesn't require any more intelligence, knowledge, or skill than you probably already have. What it does require is patience, self-discipline, effort, and the willingness to display your writing ability.

For an outline of your written report, consider the outline in Figure 12.4 when preparing your presentation.

Whichever presentation you use — written or verbal, detailed or summarized — it will be dramatically enhanced by illustrations, graphs, films, statements from others, statistics, and other aids. Never underestimate the importance of visual presentations. Marketing research states that people retain 10 percent of what they hear, 35 percent of what they see, and 65 percent of what they *see and hear*.

Figure 12.4

Problem situation	(Something is wrong).
Problem definition	(What you believe the problem is).
Problem objectives	(What you wish to achieve by implementing your solution).
Consequences of putting solution into action.	(Tactful discussion of the more likely objections to be raised).
Various options for implementing the solution	(List various ways of putting your solution into effect).
Selected implementation	(Discuss why you have chosen a particular way of implementing your solution).
Decision	(Request what you want: for example; money, time, further study of your idea, etc.).
Implementing solution	(What you plan to do if the idea is approved).

Action!

Many ideas are rejected. You have to anticipate such a response even to your most cherished solution. Someone else may be better able to determine whether an idea is good. Know when to stop selling a solution. There is little to be gained from being persistent with people who will not be persuaded. Wearing them down achieves nothing, except antagonism, which may cause greater difficulties in the long run. Now let's turn to questions you'll need to answer if your solution is accepted.

• What are ways you can put your idea into effect?

• Who should do each step?

• Where should these be done?

• Where is the best place to do these?

• How should these be done?

Many ideas fail not because the concept is weak, but because of the way the idea is presented to others. You have to think creatively to prepare for the difficulties you may face when you attempt to carry out an idea. Creative and thorough planning encourages better ideas and more successful solutions to every-day problems.

Before you put your solution to work, you need to have all the facts about it. Then you must plan how you will "sell" your solution to others. If you spend most of your time finding solutions and too little on making use of them, you may feel that putting ideas into action is too troublesome, or you simply overlook this part of the problem-solving process. It's foolish to spend so much time coming up with a good solution, and then fail to carry it out because you lack an effective implementation strategy.

BIBLIOGRAPHY

Smith, Emily T. 1985. "Are You Creative?" *Business Week*, September 30.

Dyer, Wayne. 1976. *Your Erroneous Zones*. New York: Funk & Wagnalls.

Hocking, Ernest. 1912. *The Meaning of God in Human Experience: A Philosophic Study of Religion*. Yale University Press.

Guilford, J.P. 1977. *Way Beyond the IQ*. New York: The Creative Education Foundation.

Hoffer, Eric. 1962. *The Ordeal of Change*.

Janis, Irving. 1982. *Groupthink*, 2nd ed. Boston: Houghton-Mifflin Co.

Kepner, C.H., and Tregoe, B.B. 1965. *The Rational Manager*. New York: McGraw-Hill.

Knaus, William. 1979. *Do it Now*. Englewood Cliffs, NJ: Prentice-Hall.

Lyles, Richard. 1982. *Practical Management Problem Solving*. New York: Van Nostrand-Reinhold Co.

Olsen, Robert. 1980. *The Art of Creative Thinking*. New York: Harper-Row.

Paolucci, Beatrice. 1977. *Family Decision Making: An Ecosystem Approach*. New York: John Wiley & Sons.

Sanderson, Michael. 1979. *Successful Problem Management*. New York: John Wiley & Sons.

Toffler, Alvin. 1970. *Future Shock*. New York: Random House.

Walford, Roy. *Maximum Life Span*. 1983. New York: W.W. Norton and Company.